BUSINESS ADVISOR PLAYBOOK

SELL YOUR ADVICE
VOLUME 1

AMANDA C. WATTS

Business Advisor Playbook Volume 1
First Published in 2024

This book is not intended to provide personalised legal, financial or investment advice. The author specifically disclaims any liability, loss or risk which is incurred as a consequence, directly or indirectly of the use and application of any of the content of this work.

Author: Amanda C. Watts

All rights reserved. No part of this publication may be reproduced, distributed, or transmitted in any form or by any means, including photocopying, recording, or other electronic or mechanical methods, without the prior written permission of the author, except in the case of brief quotations embodied in reviews and certain other non-commercial uses permitted by copyright law.

Your work is going to fill a large part of your life, and the only way to be truly satisfied is to do what you believe is great work.

And the only way to do great work is to love what you do.

STEVE JOBS

CONTENTS

Introduction		1
Chapter 1	The Game Of Being A Business Advisor	12
Chapter 2	How To Show The Value Of Your Advisory Offering	22
Chapter 3	What Is Your Role As A Business Advisor	30
Chapter 4	How To Do Content Marketing And Attract High Value Clients	38
Chapter 5	Business Coaches Are Stealing Your Advisory Clients	50
Chapter 6	The 4 Stages Of Becoming Vital	60
Chapter 7	How To Fire Toxic Clients	70
Chapter 8	6 Elements Of Building A Personal Brand	84
Chapter 9	5 Ways To Sell More Advisory	100
Chapter 10	Conquering Imposter Syndrome	116
Chapter 11	The Secret To Building An Audience Fast	130
Chapter 12	How I Structure My Time In My Practice	144
Chapter 13	5 Reasons Your Clients Will Choose You	164

Chapter 14	The One Where I Lost 1 Million Pounds	176
Chapter 15	The One Where You Become The 1%	194
Chapter 16	The One About How Not To Be Questioned On Price	210
Chapter 17	How To Create A Loyal Community That Wants To Buy From You	226
Chapter 18	Create Your 10x Vision To Guide You	244
Chapter 19	How To Run An Advisory Session Using The Grow Model	261
Chapter 20	How I Beat My Own Doubts (And How You Can Too)	286

Next Steps	304
About Amanda C. Watts	307
About The Business Advisor Academy	308

INTRODUCTION

As I compiled the information for the Business Advisor Podcast (this is what this Playbook is based on) I experienced a huge rollercoaster of emotions.

From fear, anger and frustration, through to joy, excitement, and an eagerness to share.

You see, I've been running my own business since 2009 now and I'm happy to admit I've made a lot of mistakes in that time.

But one mistake stands out head and shoulders above the rest.

This mistake has meant I've spent most of my entrepreneurial years overworked, with limited personal income and watching my business going backwards rather than moving forward.

The reason? I was using an OLD (Overworked, Limited, and Demoralising) model.

A few years ago I scaled an agency to circa £1.5 million in revenue. I had a large team, a business with lots of moving parts, and we were doing all the work for our clients with little to no appreciation and – more importantly – with little profit. We had what I call a "Monster Business".

To improve matters, I decided to offer some coaching and advisory packages, which I quickly took to 120k a month with a 55% profit margin. However, in truth, my business model still had a bloated team and too many moving parts.

The problem?

By following the OLD business model, I built the wrong business. One that was big, complex, fast-paced, overwhelming, and that offered low margins. I became a slave to marketing and hated it. It was a case of too much hustle and very little fun.

If you're currently running a professional service firm, I'm guessing this might sound all too familiar.

However, fast forward to today, and you'll find me running a streamlined "one core offer, to one core audience, to one core result" model.

I call this new model "the Freedom Practice".

And, since I discovered it, everything's changed.

More importantly, it's helped my clients' business models change, too; meaning they now generate advisory revenue of 500k (profits of 70% or more) whilst client delivery has moved down to less than 10 hours a week. (And have managed to free themselves from compliance work.)

OLD MODEL

- High revenue
- Tons of staff
- Hundreds of clients
- Loads of hours in client delivery
- Low profit margin
- Small take-home pay
- Compliance-based

FREEDOM PRACTICE (NEW MODEL)

- High take-home pay
- Small intimate team
- High-value clients
- 10 hours a week in client delivery
- High-profit margin
- High retention, high lifetime-value
- Simple, fun, full of freedom
- Almost empty calendar, leaving you free to do the things you really want to do.

In a nutshell, my Freedom Practice model is the best and most complete system I've seen for business advisors; one that offers more free time, little to no stress, and financial freedom.

We call this model the 500:10 Model - which is 500k in revenue and 10 hours of client delivery a week.

THE FAIRY TALE FADES

Once upon a time, the accounting profession was highly respected and when young adults finished college it was considered one of the best professions to join. It set practitioners up with a great career, and with a guaranteed income that would enable them to live the good life ...

Until, that is, it didn't.

Instead, we found ourselves working all the hours under the sun, having to work with thousands of different clients, and every year tax season would be the bane of our life.

In a double whammy, we also faced a shift in attitude from business owners. Digital software came along and they started to think they didn't need an accountant as much.

Accountants were no longer seen as a mysterious entity essential to business. Instead, we became a cost.

People started questioning us on price and simply to choose the cheapest.

Our value dipped dramatically.

However, the majority of accountants continued to offer the same service. We had been trained to do the same as the accountant next to us and to each and every accountant that came before. We had become a commoditised profession.

Sadly, as much of the world was evolving, the accounting profession stayed the same, doing things in the same OLD way.

Let me share a story with you:

A young woman is preparing a ham for a family dinner. As she's about to place it in the roasting pan, she instinctively cuts off both ends before placing it in the pan. Her husband, curious, asks her why. The young woman responds that her mother always did it that way, so she does too.

Intrigued, the husband decides to call the young woman's mother to ask why she always cut off both ends of the ham. The mother replies that she learned it from her own mother, the young woman's grandmother.

Determined to get to the bottom of things, the husband finally calls the grandmother to ask the same question. The grandmother's answer is revealing: she cut off the ends because her roasting pan was too small to fit the whole ham.

This fable reminds me of the way in which many accountancy firms are still run today: offering a mostly compliance-based service and charging by the hour (thereby creating hugely complex businesses with large teams that are monsters to run). And to this day new owners are setting up accounting firms in exactly the same way that they were 100 years ago.

Which leads me to this well-known saying from the founder of the Ford Motor Company, Henry Ford: "If I had asked people what they wanted, they would have said faster horses."

Henry Ford radically changed the way we think about innovation. At the time, horses were still the main mode of transport. If he had listened to what people asked for, it's likely that they would indeed have said they wanted faster horses.

But Ford understood that sometimes customers don't know exactly what they need until they see it. So instead of simply making small improvements, he brought motor cars to the masses.

Remember, real innovation often comes from understanding deeper needs, even if these aren't explicitly stated. It's about thinking beyond what's familiar and imagining what might be possible – perhaps, like Ford, changing the world in the process.

***

One reason the story of Ford resonates so much with me is that I genuinely believe that creating a Freedom Practice is what so many of you need to do to achieve the success you deserve.

But if, for example, I asked you right now to name your firm's biggest problems, I'm sure you'd say: I need a larger team; or, I just need to sort out my business systems; or, I need to improve the software we use.

In other words, you're looking to make your horse go faster when in fact what you need is a completely new model – the motor car.

And that – for those in the professional services sector – is exactly what I've created.

Many people still think the more hours they put in, the more money they'll make. Or the bigger their team, the more successful they are. Or the more they hustle, the more they'll be rewarded.

Well, I've flipped this idea on its head and can tell you it has nothing to do with money, and everything to do with being VITAL.

It's about creating one core successful offering; one that sets you apart from every other accountant and business advisor and guarantees a massive transformation for your clients.

After all, clients don't care about how much work you do, but about the transformation *you bring*.

Currently, though, the profession has got out of whack. Like the daughter, it's still chopping the ends off the ham and throwing them in the bin. By focusing on the wrong things, it's creating faster horses rather than the motor car – and all because we were told that this was the way to run a firm.

I know this is true because by now I've worked incredibly closely with over 700 professional service firms, and all bar a few were still following the traditional OLD (remember, that's Overworked, Limited, and Decaying) model.

That's why things have got to change. They've reached a tipping point and it's time to shake up the whole profession – which is what this book sets out to do.

The ideas I'm going to share go directly against what traditional firms have been doing for centuries.
Some of you, then, will read the lessons I offer and dismiss them without a second thought. Others will embrace them and run all the way to the bank.

But please don't imagine I made them up, especially for this book. It's important you know that I've been helping business owners change their models and reap huge benefits from doing so since 2016.

Some have introduced an advisory offering but still offer compliance to support their advice-giving. Some have sold their compliance clients and completely stopped offering compliance as a service.

While others have shut down their firm to become a "business coach", meaning they no longer talk about just finance, but the mindset, time management, and HR to name a few other skills!

All of my clients who've embraced the Freedom Practice model have been through an evolution – of their mindset, their income, their time off, and their freedom. And all from changing one thing: their business model.

Are you ready to explore with me? Come on, let's dive in...

Turn the page for Chapter 1 - The Game Of Being A Business Advisor

CHAPTER 1
THE GAME OF BEING A BUSINESS ADVISOR

Let's take a moment to talk about the big picture and the business advisory game that you play.

At the simplest and most mechanical level, this is about a life and business you design for yourself.

From your point of view, it is about stepping out of the "doing" for your clients and moving into the "advising" of your clients. It's about working with people that you like in a way that gives you freedom.

From an output point of view, by being a business advisor in a practice, there is an opportunity for you to earn half a million only working 10 hours a week in delivery with 1 or 2 staff.

It is possible and doable and has been done many times around the world. Any belief that it is something that you cannot do is just going on inside your head.

The game is one where you take your three strengths (financial expertise, the everyday knowledge that you have, and who you are), and package them up. Then you sell your advice.

This is where you can make an income that transforms your life, and have an impact that transforms other people's lives.

This game is a game of courage. It means stepping away from the traditional way of running your business and making the shift to running a practice.

It is going from being underpaid and overworked to financial freedom and more time in your personal life.

It is going from a Monster Business to a Freedom Practice.

The Monster Business consists of hundreds of clients where you are doing all the work for them, paying yourself last, and growing a team. On top of that, you have certain vampire clients sucking the life out of you. Lastly, you are working 40-60 hour weeks.

A Freedom Practice has 10-50 clients, involves advising people around the numbers and their business growth/strategy, paying yourself first, having a small team of 1-2 people, and working with great people that you want to talk to—all in 10 hours a week of delivery...

It is where you go from being a commodity and doing the same as everyone else, to standing out, having a voice, and sharing your experience.

It is about shifting in all aspects of your career. You will shift from a task-oriented perspective to a people-centric one. You will no longer be doing. You will instead be guiding. Nothing involves fixing. It is all about empowering your clients. Gone are the performance evaluations. The new focus is growth support. The fixed mindset is replaced with the growth mindset. You are no longer the technician. You are the advisor.

Our logo at the Business Advisor Academy - the lion - is not just something that a random designer chose for us. The idea to use the lion as the symbol in the Business Advisor Academy evolved from my childhood. When I was young, I was a big fan of The Lion, the Witch and the Wardrobe. In fact, I still am. I find the movie terribly moving. I read all the books, too.

Aslan (the lion) was fierce. He represents courage, strength, and goodness. He is seen as a protector and saviour.

The side of Aslan I felt that was most powerful was his role as a guide to the children, and how he became their friend. Aslan was quiet and patient. It was never about him. It was about the greater good. He had a different perspective and foresight; a vision for goodness and to serve others.

Many of you will, at this point, want to shout out and say, "Yes, but Aslan represents Christ and the Church". This is not the reason the story was so powerful for me. As a child, it was his goodness and kindness, and how he empowered the children, and the whole of Narnia, to believe in themselves. He was a leader.

Just as a business advisor needs to be. You will need to embody the strength, wisdom, and empathy of a lion. Empowerment, empathy, and bringing change are what your clients are seeking from you.

Your job as a business advisor is to package, sell, and deliver your advice for the greater good. You will be working with clients, so they can have their life and business by design. The more value you bring, the more valuable you are. The more valuable you are, the wealthier you will become.

The goal is for you to be generating at least 500k in billings. The breakdown is as follows:

- 100k will be allocated for costs

- 300k-400k will come to you and your family, which will be taxed accordingly and leave you around 200k.

You will stop doing the work for people and start empowering your clients to understand and do the work for themselves.

This works across most countries. We are benchmarked to the USA and UK with 1 pound equaling 2 dollars. 500k British pounds equals 1 million US dollars. This works for when you charge for your services, too. Here in the UK, 1000 pounds a month for advisory work is a good ballpark figure to start with; in the USA it's 2000 dollars a month.

This business is a dichotomy. It's not about the money, and it is all about the money. Money provides security. When someone is secure they come from a good place. If you are struggling financially, worrying constantly, and living in anxiety, you can't show up as the leader, advisor, or mentor that you have been put on this earth to be.

Naturally, we would all like to say that we love what we do so much that we would do it for free, but if we did it for free, our ability to make a difference would be short-lived.

Money gives income and impact. It gives you the chance to live your life to the fullest. Additionally, it gives you the chance to help others live their life that way, as well

The thing that is different about running a Freedom Practice from a Monster Business is that it allows you to live your life to the fullest now, and not wait for the day you sell your business or retire and get your pension.

If you could take the next 3 years to generate a revenue of 200k after taxes and live relatively lean, you would be able to invest that money in property or stocks and shares. It would be an investment that grows in value.

With everything that has happened in the world in the past few years, and the speed of change in business, technology, and life, being an advisor has never been more important than it is now. It is time for you to stand up and help more people. Come out from behind your computer and make a difference!

If you play the game of the 500:10 model - 500k of advisory revenue in 10 hours a week in delivery - to get from where you are to there, you have to start with little projects.

These projects change as you build your practice, but it starts with creating the right offering (we call it an Offer Diamond). Next, it is about shifting your position in the marketplace by using a signature methodology. It is about being known for the advice you give, and then it's about building the practice by design in a way that sits in alignment with your dreams.

Over 90-day periods, you run campaigns to add 1-3 new clients a month, They will be paying you 500-2k or more a month for your services. Over a 1-3 year period, you add 500k+ in revenue to your Freedom Practice.

Having played this game for several decades, I know this is a fundamental shift in identity. There is a change in how you see yourself and how the world sees you. The difference between a technician and an advisor is that a technician is not known in their own right, they just do some work for people. In contrast, an advisor is known for knowing stuff in their own right and is looked up to as an expert.

The core of the identity shift is a move from being a faceless business to being known and respected in your own right.

It's less about how big a business you can have. Stop thinking it's all about systems and teams, and shift your thinking to how much value you can bring the world. You will get paid for that value.

This shift is often a journey of rediscovery and growth. It can be hard to even comprehend moving to advisory as a full-time gig without having to do the work for clients. What I do know for sure is that your confidence grows the more you show up, and you create and form who you are as you go on this journey and the difference you can make on the planet.

If you show up in service to others, you start to experience a shift in fulfilment and meaning; in happiness and contribution. It goes from the stress of you running a Monster Business with no one coming to save you, to shifting to a Freedom Practice model where you are in it with others, and have a tribe of people wanting you to succeed and have your back.

Think about how you would feel if you could pull yourself out of doing the work and being in the weeds all the time, to being the advisor. You will be both empowering others and having the income and impact you truly desire...

CHAPTER 2
HOW TO SHOW THE VALUE OF YOUR ADVISORY OFFERING

Before we get into anything with too much detail, there is a very simple proposition at the heart of your Advisory/CFO journey. You are going to think of something that you know helps business owners, and you are going to help them with it.

It can be so easy to overthink what being an advisor is. It can be a scary thought when you have probably been caught up being a technician for the whole of your adult life; doing the work for your clients and being behind the scenes.

I want you to come back to this very simple proposition: Think of something you know that helps someone else and share it with them. The way we do that is with our *Offer Diamond*.

The *Offer Diamond* is a strategy that precisely targets the right audience with a clear and appealing solution that meets a specific need.

When you have the right offer, several things occur:

- Enhanced client engagement
- An increase in the perceived value of your services (Transformational, not transactional)
- Financial success for you
- Client satisfaction

The heart of your *Offer Diamond* is something we call the *Signature System*. This is your unique methodology, where you take someone from the pain they are in and provide them with the solution that they want or desire... a *Signature System* enables you to show the real value behind your work with a client.

If the *Signature System* is the heart of what you are presenting the client with, the *Offer Diamond* is how you present that solution, along with the explanation of how you are going to deliver it.

A diamond represents quality, highly perceived value, brilliance, and uniqueness. Exactly what you want your offer to be.

It shows your quality, the high value you are bringing, and your brilliance. It makes you unique from everyone else in the marketplace.

An *Offer Diamond* has five points. Let's look at them closely:

Point 1. A Clear Outcome
This is where we have to know what success looks like for your client. For us, we talk about adding 500k in advisory services in the next 1-3 years and delivering this advisory offering in less than 10 hours a week. This is what success looks like for our clients.

Point 2. A Specific Timeframe
It is really important to set a timeframe so that clients can make a decision based on how long you think it will take for them to get the results they want. It is important to set realistic timeframes or people will get frustrated. We have had clients add 1 million pounds to their accounting business in a little over a year, but our offer is 500k in 1-3 years, as making money that fast is not typical. However, adding 100k in 12 weeks is not unheard of. Neither is 500k in 18 months, which is the average of our go-getters.

Point 3. The Right Price
Under-price and you will create yourself a Vampire Client. You will have the life sucked out of you, and you will find yourself resenting the client. Overprice and you will have unhappy clients, or even no clients at all. The value just isn't there for them to buy from you.

Pricing is a mixture of several things, and one of the things that affect how much you charge is your confidence. It is not unusual for clients that work with us to gradually increase their price with every new client, and as their confidence grows.

It may sound exciting to be able to charge 3k a month for your advisory services, but for many people, charging nearly 40k a year for their services might feel like a full-time job when it is not. So you start smaller than your value, but higher enough that you feel a little uncomfortable.

Point 4. Offer To The Right Person
Knowing who is the best client for your services will make the sale much easier. If you are providing an advisory/fractional CFO offering, you want to work with people who need this offer. These people have to be able to afford you, be able to need you, and be someone you like. There is no point in working with people you do not like. This is often forgotten when trying to decide on a target market.

Ideally, for high-value CFO and advisory services, you want to work with a business that has a revenue of at least 250-500k or more and has a need outside of the basic technician/compliance work.

Point 5. Deliver In The Right Way

There are six delivery mechanisms - Coach, Advisor, Facilitator, Trainer, Author, and Speaker. The way you deliver your paid-for advisory offering will be a mixture of all of them. You need to work out how that is going to look.

Ask yourself these questions:

- Are you going to work with clients locally or globally?
- Are you going to do live or pre-recorded training to back up your advisory delivery?
- Are you going to work with clients offline or online?
- Are you going to take clients on at any time, or are you going to use a launch strategy?
- Are you working with clients for a short time, or will it be ongoing year after year?

So many options...

Here is a look at a couple of offers my clients have created:

- Nishi created a program called Apex. It is delivered face to face, and he holds group planning sessions once a quarter as a main part of his advisory offering.

- Jane offers her services through online pre-recorded training sessions and then has Q&A sessions regularly. These sessions help her clients overcome any challenges, and she can answer questions that may arise.

There are so many options that you can choose from. Your advisory offer should be a good fit for you and your client.

Remember that YOU are at the heart of your offer. You are advising about something that you know to people who need your help.

CHAPTER 3
WHAT IS YOUR ROLE AS A BUSINESS ADVISOR?

There is a fundamental shift when you make the move from a technician to an advisor. The shift goes from doing the work for your clients to advising clients on how they can have the outcomes they want.

As a financial professional, you are in an envious position. Unlike many business owners, what you know is both life and business-changing.

What do I mean by this?

Well, as a financial professional, you get to move the needle on the most important currency for opportunity—money. You get to help people see how much they have, how much they need, and how to get (or save) more.

Your experience in growing a business based on the numbers means that not only can you advise around numbers, but you can also advise around things you have learned on the way. The way you decide on the advice you give clients will be a mixture between your experience, your education, and the essence of you.

Once you have a little bit of clarity around these three things, you can then start to analyze your ideal client.

Your focus is to find out what the client wants help in achieving.

A really good advisor embodies the mindset and actions of a Sherpa. Growing a business is like climbing a mountain. Both are treacherous. The weather can change, the ground can fall from under you, and you can reach a block in the journey where you have to turn back and try a different way. In both situations, clients are looking for guidance through rough terrain.

This is where the magic happens. This is where you become a Sherpa. You will help your clients climb up the mountain and reach the summit of success.

Just like a Sherpa, there are certain things that your clients will need from you. They come in the form of five crucial elements.

Those elements are:

1. **Helping to analyze** their current situation.
2. **Providing support** preparing and planning for their success.
3. **Managing risks** in regards to changes in the market, the economy, and within the businesses themselves.
4. **Enhancing the client's skills** and providing training in the way of the business world.
5. **Giving support and motivation.**

These elements can be combined into what we call the Success Triad.

The components of the Triad are as follows:

- **Navigate**—Navigation covers the current situation and how risks should be managed.
- **Elevate**—Elevation is about preparing and planning for your client's success.
- **Support**—Ongoing support and motivation are crucial for sustained growth and success.

Every advisor needs to ensure they have the *Success Triad* in place—and then leverage the *Triad* to create a bespoke signature system for their clients.

In Chapter Two, we spoke about the *Offer Diamond*, and how you articulate your offer. Along with the *Offer Diamond*, I mentioned an important tool called the *Signature System*.

A *Signature System* is a roadmap that clearly shows the steps you take with clients to help them reach the summit of the mountain. It is the step-by-step actions your clients need to take to have the success they are looking for.

What you include in your *Signature System*, and the logistics inside of the *Success Triad*, will depend on you and your client.

In the Business Advisor Academy, we focus on creating the *Signature System*, as it is the foundation of your advisory practice. Such a foundation saves hours of time and effort as you launch and scale your advisory offers.

Once completed, your *Signature System* will enable you to cut through the noise of online marketing. It will ensure you have a clear vision of how you help your clients. It will give your clients complete clarity and confidence that you know what you are talking about, and it will ensure that you articulate your value in a way that has a long line of people wanting to work with you.

(Let's not forget that they will pay you handsomely in the process.)

I want you to imagine the exact things your ideal client needs to have in place for success. For example, if your ideal clients are plumbers, they will need something completely different from a client who is involved in e-commerce. This is why it is important to know who exactly your client base is.

Now, I want you to list out everything that an ideal client has to have, do, and be to reach their goals.

You may struggle with this, especially if you do not have a clear understanding of what your clients want. But once you have worked out your ideal client, and got to grips with their problems, creating a *Signature System* can be much easier.

The key framework is to look at where they are now, where they want to be, and the gap between those two points. That gap is your methodology, and your job is to fill the gap.

When you think about being an advisor, and wonder what an advisor does, the answer lies in what your clients want.

It's not so much about you, but more about them. Where are they now, where do they want to be, and what is the gap? You then take your experience, your education, and your essence to bridge the gap.

The idea is to help them navigate, elevate them, and provide support.

CHAPTER 4
HOW TO DO CONTENT MARKETING AND ATTRACT HIGH-VALUE CLIENTS

Now, we're diving into a topic that's a game changer when marketing your business advisory services. Content Marketing. I'm not just going to talk about its effectiveness; I'm going to show you how to use it, correctly and powerfully. Let's get started with the first and most important question:

What is content marketing?

Content marketing is a strategic marketing approach focused on creating and distributing valuable, relevant, and consistent content to attract and retain a clearly defined audience. Ultimately, it is the approach you use to get people to buy from you and purchase the right product at the right price–all done while eliminating tire kickers and repelling vampire clients.

By the way, it may be a good time to note how content marketing has been pivotal in my making over 5 million pounds in the past 10 years. It has enabled me to hire an outstanding team, along with giving me a great reputation and helping me become a key player in the accounting profession as a marketing and sales expert.

I have recorded over 800 videos, written over 1000 blog articles, and have run over 1000 webinars. I post on social media almost daily, and now I have a weekly podcast, as well.

I have also written three best-selling books. *ESCAPE - the Definitive Guide to Escaping the Rat Race* helps people escape their corporate jobs. *Practice Growth Super Powers for Accountants and Bookkeepers*, along with *The Pioneering Practice*, are great examples of content marketing.

My fourth book, Business Advisor Playbook, is what you are reading now. Additionally, I am mapping out book number five, which is all about getting stuff done and coming out of overwhelming circumstances.

If you are wondering, "Why should we listen to Amanda when it comes to content marketing?", my results from marketing should showcase it. My use of content marketing has enabled me to buy my dream house and my dream car and take wonderful vacations with my family. Thanks to my success in the field, I have a strong personal brand, a voice, and a way to make an impact.

But you might be saying, "Yeah, but Amanda, it's easy for you—you are a marketer".

Yes, I agree. I do get a lot of pleasure out of content marketing and find it quite easy, but that is not because I am a marketer. It is because I focus on helping my ideal clients and providing them with a valuable service.

I have worked with many accountants and CFOs who fall under the category of left-brained, not right-brained (meaning they are more technical-minded rather than creative). Even though these individuals are more technical, they find creating content much easier when approaching content marketing from a place of service.

Kristina, for example, built a database of over 20,000 subscribers. She sends a newsletter every week and runs webinars almost weekly.

Kevin, one of my "introvert" accountants, challenged himself to record 100 days of videos.

Sally creates Instagram reels a few times a week. Like Kevin, she also challenged herself to create 100 days of videos.

A year ago, neither of them would have even conceived of it.

As with all of the shifts involved in going from technician to advisor, you have to shift your mindset. You have to switch from doing stuff to just get clients, to doing stuff that serves prospects. The by-product of serving prospects is that you get clients.

The current trend that is working so very well for my clients is the increase in personalized and niche-focused content. This approach involves tailoring content specifically to target segments of the market, rather than using a one-size-fits-all strategy. Business advisors are now focusing more on creating content that speaks directly to the specific needs, challenges, and interests of their target audience. This personalization can be based on various factors such as industry (e.g., content tailored for small business owners, nonprofits, or specific sectors like technology or healthcare), business size, or even the stage in the business lifecycle.

Niching is a big topic, so I don't want you to overthink it right now. What I do want to touch on is the power of niching when creating content. For example, a business advisor might produce in-depth content for startups on managing finances in the early stages, or for established companies looking into international expansion.

This specialization not only showcases the firm's expertise in a particular area, but also helps in attracting clients who are looking for advisors with specific knowledge and experience.

Very importantly, you must steer clear of technical content, especially on social media. There is little interaction, and your clients don't understand your terminology. My advice, along with the data results from clients, shows that covering broad financial strategies, tax planning, regulatory changes, and even business growth tips, get regular interaction— even more so when personalized.

The goal is to position you, or your practice, as a valuable resource and advisor—not just a service provider. You want people to bookmark your content, binge-watch it, and consume it like they consume a Netflix documentary. This is when you know your content is working.

Hugely successful business advisors are increasingly adopting various multimedia formats like videos, podcasts, and webinars. These formats can make something complex seem more accessible and engaging. Interactive content, such as online calculators or self-assessment tools, is also gaining traction.

You will hear me use the phrase "sell your advice". The best way to entice someone to buy your advice is to lead with free thought leadership. Establishing such leadership is done through in-depth articles, white papers, and industry reports. These are all key trends we are seeing.

Many clients are writing their own books in 2024. This type of content helps in building credibility. Being an author positions you as the "go-to" advisor for a prospect.

Let's break down what content marketing involves:

The first step is content creation. This includes blog posts, videos, podcasts, infographics, eBooks, webinars, and more. The content should provide value to your target audience. It involves answering their questions, solving their problems, or enriching their knowledge.

A great book I read on my content journey was a book by Marcus Sheridan called *They Ask, You Answer*. When I read the book I wanted to cry. It was the book I always wanted to write. I highly recommend you get yourself a copy. It is so good!

The underlying message is, "What questions are your clients asking you, or what questions are your prospects asking you?"

When you are clear on those questions, use content marketing to answer them.

Content marketing is so powerful because, when done well, it is both relevant and valuable to the world. Unlike traditional advertising, which often interrupts the audience, content marketing provides information that the audience finds useful. This could be educational content, informative articles, entertaining videos, et cetera, that relate to what the audience is interested in. This not only helps people but positions you as an expert. Therefore, your perceived value increases.

It is extremely important to be consistent with your content marketing. Regularly delivering content keeps your audience engaged and helps build a relationship with them.

Consistency in style, tone, and delivery is also key to establishing brand recognition and trust. I am known for my enthusiasm, and I have been told that I inspire people.

This is one of the reasons I wanted to start my podcast. I would be able to reach and inspire even more people!

You are responsible for knowing who your 'people' are when you are writing or recording your content marketing. You need to understand your ideal audience, and know their preferences, pain points, challenges, and what questions they are seeking answers to.

The ultimate goal of content marketing is to influence customer behavior toward profitable actions. This could be signing up for a newsletter, making a purchase, downloading a guide, etc. My favorite call to action is getting people to come to a webinar.

Over time, delivering consistent, high-quality content establishes your brand. Along with the establishment of your brand, you are now thought of as a leader or expert in your field. This builds trust with your audience, making them more likely to choose your products or services when they are ready to buy.

When I speak with business advisors, I often address their concerns regarding giving away free information. My clients come to me for assurance that they won't lose out on business because their content marketing gives away too much.

A breakdown of audience types helps clarify what is going on concerning how their potential audience reacts to what is being offered.

Your audience typically falls into one of three categories:

- **Group One:** Serial Freebie Hunters They're not your ideal clients, since they don't intend to purchase.
- **Group Two:** Potential Clients These are people who will try to do things themselves, but they might eventually seek expert help if they don't achieve the desired results.
- **Group Three:** Goldmine Clients. They prefer not to dabble and seek expert help right off the bat. These individuals value time and quality and are willing to pay for it.

Your goal with content marketing should be to target these latter two groups. Provide them with content that showcases your expertise, and when they're ready to seek professional services, your business will be at the forefront of their minds. It's all about building that trust and authority in your niche.

A critical piece of advice I always give: prioritize quality over quantity. The internet is flooded with content, but not all of it is helpful or valuable. Your content should stand out by being insightful, informative, and genuinely useful to your audience.

In conclusion, content marketing is an incredibly powerful tool. It's not just about creating content; it's about creating the right content for the right audience and establishing a connection. Remember, in the long run, it's the value you provide that turns readers/listeners into clients. Embrace this strategy, and watch as it transforms your advisory practice. You have to create valuable free content if you want to attract better clients; better clients need to see your value before they invest with you. This is the power of content marketing.

To get you started with your content marketing journey we have created something called the Content Vault.

It is specifically for business advisors who want to show up as thought leaders online, and give advice around business growth. There are over 300 blog articles and 500 social media posts.

Training on how to take a blog article and turn it into a video or podcast is also available.

If I do say so myself it is an awesome product...and right now we have it at a very special offer. Check it out at https://go.oompf.global/the-content-vault.

If you want to do content marketing in less than 30 minutes a week, then this is for you. Grab it now while it is still available.

CHAPTER 5
BUSINESS COACHES ARE STEALING YOUR ADVISORY CLIENTS

The topic of how business coaches are stealing advisory clients is something I feel very passionate about. There needs to be a talk about how we need to shift your mindset, so you stop missing out on huge opportunities because you are using the wrong language.

Everywhere I look, you are being told that you need to position yourself as a business advisor or trusted advisor. Heck, even I am doing it! My business is called the Business Advisor Academy. However, I would confidently say that 80% of the world has no idea what a business advisor is or does for their clients.

Outside of the financial accounting/tax world, the word business advisor is not used. Which, in turn, makes it very difficult for you to sell something that nobody knows they need. The number one thing that makes an easy sell is someone knowing they have a problem and being aware of who they need to hire to help them fix it.

Sadly, this is why accountants and financial experts get less traction than they deserve when it comes to selling advisory. No one knows that they need a business advisor to help them overcome any pain (or meet any aspirations) that they have in their business.

Business owners tend to think they have a business problem, so they look for a business COACH to help them. I bet now, if you went to the profit and loss accounts of your clients on Xero or Quickbooks, and looked at the expenditure of your clients, you would have a monthly line item that says consultancy or coaching. This line item will be anywhere between 500 to 5k pounds or dollars a month.

Now, when you see this line item that says business coaching/consulting, I want you to get a little bit angry. I want you to think for a moment that your clients have chosen to pay someone else–who is probably not qualified and has never run a business before. They are paying them a lot of money for something you could do better.

That 6k to 60k a year that a business coach is pocketing is probably going to the wrong person. That person is not able to help them as much as you can, as they don't have their fingers on the FINANCIAL pulse like you do.

Honestly, I have worked with business coaches who have no idea how to manage their own money; they have been unable to pay their tax bills because they haven't been able to read the numbers. Yet people still invest in them to help with their business! It's just complete madness... I've done it myself! In the past, I paid business coaches as much as 5k a month for their advice. Unfortunately, the advice given was fluffy, non-specific, and of little help.

The strength of one particular business coach I paid was, in fact, the community that they had built. This is where I found their value. It was the insights and experiences of like-minded entrepreneurs that made it worthwhile.

Building a community of business owners is something that a business advisor can do. It is one of six delivery mechanisms that we will be talking about in an upcoming chapter.

However, before getting sidetracked, I am going to focus again on making sure that business coaches don't steal your clients.

As financial professionals, you are used to thinking that your competitors are other CPAs, accountants, bookkeepers, and the like. The shift to an advisory capacity takes these people out of the key competition.

Business coaches are who you should be looking at if you want to step into the CFO/advisory arena. Maybe you should be calling yourself a business coach, instead of a business advisor, as this is what potential clients are looking for at networking events, on Google, in Facebook Groups, and on LinkedIn.

The name change will be a secret weapon in your arsenal. It is a strategic advantage that, if leveraged correctly, isn't just going to nudge you ahead of the competition—it's going to launch you into a league of your own. Imagine a world where you're not just competing, but completely redefining the game.

Let's get real about business coaching. It's a booming industry with quite a mix of talent levels. Some have incredible talent, some are middle-of-the-road players, and a fair share are not-so-stellar coaches. The market's bursting at the seams because the entry barrier is almost nonexistent. Anybody can wake up and call themselves a business coach; no rigorous training or credentials are needed. It's easier than setting up a lemonade stand!

How do you, as a financial expert, make your mark in this 'business advisory' arena? How do you shine brighter than the rest?

Many of you hesitate to step into this role due to self-doubt and uncertainty about your ability to effectively provide these services. I'm going to share a couple of tips and strategies to help you realize that you do have this and that you can confidently compete with other business coaches.

First up, let's talk about customized advice. Unlike generic business coaching, financial pros like yourself bring a treasure trove of industry-specific knowledge, and you can make your advice incredibly relevant and impactful. Imagine advice that's not just tailored to a business, but aligns with the latest industry trends and regulatory requirements. That's what an accountant brings to the table. That's what YOU bring to the table through your experience, expertise, and personal essence.

You can integrate the financial health of the business into every recommendation, focusing on long-term strategic plans for sustainable growth. It's about building a future for your clients and their business, not just tweaking the present.

Next, let's look at zeroing in on the lifeblood of any business: cash flow.

You are financial detectives, which is shown when you can spot the inefficiencies that are draining a business' cash flow from a mile away.

It's not just about counting money like a business coach might do; you can make your clients' money work smarter. This is an advantage you have. Your advice can range from offering advanced tax efficiency strategies to creating spot-on financial forecasts. You can help anticipate and plan for future cash flow scenarios. It's about helping your clients stay ahead of the game. This 'business' game that your clients are playing is often exhausting, overwhelming, and unnerving. They need you more than you know. You are giving them peace of mind when it comes to their business finances. More than that, you are helping them with the overall feeling of security.

Now, let's get real about ROI - Return On Investment.

As an accountant, you take this to the next level with sophisticated metrics and performance indicators. You can provide detailed financial reports and set up custom dashboards for real-time financial insights. This isn't just about measuring success; it's about defining and tracking it in terms that matter to the business owner.

As an accountant and business advisor, you see in black and white the changes that will affect a bottom line. It's transparency and insight—hand in hand.

There's more to being a business advisor than the ROI, cash flow, and customized advice. You are also there as a master of risk management and compliance. You not only ensure that a business is profitable, but you can help make sure the businesses you work with are legally sound.

Let's not forget technology – you can recommend the best financial tools to streamline processes. As a business advisor, you are all about embracing efficiency and accuracy.

In conclusion, when accountants step into the role of business advisors, they bring a depth of financial expertise and a commitment to tailored and impactful business advice. You redefine what it means to be a business coach by focusing on crucial aspects like cash flow and providing measurable insights into ROI.

So, for all you financial pros out there, it's time to think beyond the traditional role. Step up and embrace your education and your experience. Then weave in the essence of you. This mixture will enable you to provide a partnership with businesses that will take them to their next level.

There is a very large chance that you have been giving all of this information for free to your clients. Maybe, in a best-case scenario, you have asked for a very small investment in return.

This needs to change.

I'm giving you one specific fact to fuel you and make you hungry to go and take the market by storm. Business coaches, who often have way less experience and education around the important financials of a business, are charging 10x what you charge for a fraction of what you deliver.

It's time for you to step up, put on the mantle, and become the leader you can be. Your competition in the marketplace is no longer just other financial professionals. Your job is to go out and own the fact that you, too, can sell your advice and be a business coach.

CHAPTER 6
THE FOUR STAGES OF BECOMING VITAL

In this chapter, I will be talking about how to position yourself as being *VITAL*. If you are not already considered *VITAL* by your clients, I will be sharing some ideas about what you will need to do.

You will hear me talk about two kinds of business models.

The first model is *The Monster Business*. It is run by OLD accountants. An OLD accountant is overworked, limited, and demoralized. (Hence the OLD acronym.)

The second model is *The Freedom Practice*. It is run by *VITAL Advisors*. They are highly valued and highly paid, attract better clients, and have more freedom in their lives.

Unlike the *OLD Accountants*, the *VITAL Advisors* are crushing it in regards to making an impact and building wealth for themselves and their clients...

Some companies are *VITAL*.

Others—not so much.

In the 1940s, Joseph Juran coined the term "The Vital Few and Trivial Many". This term came about after Juran continued the work on the 80/20 rule originally brought to us by Pareto...

Pareto observed that 80% of Italian property was owned by 20% of the Italian population.

This principle can also be applied to the fact that 80% of your income comes from 20% of your high-value clients.

The principle applies everywhere. You will also see that 20% of your time produces 80% of your results, and so on. This rule can be an incredible tool for growing the revenue of your Accounting/CPA firm.

What you need to do is figure out which 20% of your activities will produce 80% of the results you want. Likewise, by identifying which 20% of your clients represent 80% of your revenue, you can go out and find more clients like them; dramatically growing your revenue and profits.

Higher revenue + fewer clients = freedom.

A nice idea, but how easy is this to achieve?

Well, we know that the 80/20 rule can be applied to pretty much everything in life. That means that 20% of accountants are perceived as VITAL. The other 80%, unfortunately, aren't...

Let me now share with you the good news: In 2017, I carried out a survey of the accounting profession. After spending 2 years analyzing the results, and speaking with hundreds of accountants from around the world, I have determined 5 distinct characteristics that make a *VITAL Advisor*. These characteristics are:

- **Valued.** Considered to be important or beneficial; cherished.
- **Impactful.** Having a major impact or effect on the businesses they work with.
- **Trusted.** Regarded as reliable or truthful. Sought out to help the businesses they work with. A person who falls into this category is what we call The Trusted Advisor.
- **Agile.** Able to move quickly and easily, and adapt to the changes that are happening at a rapid rate. These changes happen by both the month and the year.
- **Lucrative.** Producing a great deal of profit for their clients, and subsequently making a great deal of profit for their practice.

VITAL - If you google this word, it will be described as "absolutely necessary; essential".

Let's dive in and talk about how you are going to become *VITAL*.

Well, quite simply, you must offer a better service to your clients. A service that your clients deem essential. This service is an advisory/CFO service.

Here is why this is so important:

The adage "people buy what they want, not what they need" is particularly relevant in the context of an accounting firm expanding its offerings from mere compliance to business advisory services. This shift highlights a fundamental understanding of customer psychology and market demand.

Compliance services, while necessary, are often viewed by businesses as obligatory and uninspiring. They are the needs; the essentials without which a business cannot operate legally. However, they do not stimulate growth or innovation, nor do they offer a competitive edge.

In contrast, business advisory services represent the wants.

These services cater to a business' aspirations, by offering strategies for growth, both in revenue and profit. They address the ambitions of business owners by aligning with their desires to innovate, expand, and succeed at a higher level.

When you offer business advisory services, you tap into what a client truly wants. A business owner is actively looking for help in growing the business. They want success. Sadly, compliance does not address this.

Offering advisory services capitalizes on the excitement and potential of achieving greater success for your clients. The value of success massively outweighs the mundane necessity of compliance. Being seen as a higher value to your clients translates into a higher revenue for you.

Moreover, this transition from compliance to business advisory signifies a move from a reactive to a proactive service. While compliance reacts to existing regulations, business advisory anticipates future challenges and opportunities.

A business advisor can offer tailored, forward-thinking solutions. Again, what a business owner wants.

The lesson here is to sell what people want, not what people need. People will pay more for what they want.

The journey to becoming a VITAL Advisor/CFO is a progression through four distinct stages. Each one of these stages has its own set of strategies, client relationships, and business focus. Understanding this enables you to strategically evolve your offerings and market position.

The journey starts with most firm owners in *OBSCURITY*: This first stage is where you are selling a basic compliance service to pretty much everyone you can. At this stage, you are working with any client who comes your way, regardless of fit or specialization. The focus here is getting more clients. It's about volume over value, which leads to a wide range of services being offered. Your main competitive edge is selling on price.

If you are at this stage, you are struggling to establish a market presence and a distinct identity. As I have mentioned before, you are competing primarily on cost and have no differentiation in the marketplace.

This is where so many of my new clients come to me. They are pretty frustrated and exist in the realm of *OLD*—overworked, limited, and demoralized.

Let's move on to the next stage. This is where an accountant and their firm might be seen as *VISIBLE*: The second stage is marked by a slight shift towards specialization. This is where the concept of a *'Hunting Niche®'* comes into play. Maybe you have started to identify and target a specific segment of a market, although you continue to offer a broad range of compliance services. This increased focus begins to build your reputation in a specific industry, which leads to reduced price sensitivity. This is because you are now seen as more knowledgeable or skilled in this particular niche, compared to when you were a generalist. However, at this stage, you are still a traditional accountant and are probably still struggling with OLD.

The third stage is more pronounced. This is where you are seen as *VALUED*. Now you offer niche-specific solutions, focusing exclusively on one type of client. If you are valued, your clients believe you understand them, their needs, and the challenges they face. They want your help, so they call you up.

A sad side effect is that, while the client might now start to get advisory services from you, behind the scenes you are often giving it away or charging a very minimal fee. You are still probably only getting paid pennies for your work. Additionally, you are watching your clients pay a business coach for support that you could give them yourself, or you are already giving them for free.

They do value you, but the advisory is not productized and is ad hoc, so you are not getting paid handsomely for the work.

It is still transactional, and not transformational.

But then we can move on to *VITAL*: The final stage is where you become a vital, almost indispensable, part of your clients' success. You are recognized as a Specialist Advisor/Coach. You have a deep and nuanced understanding of your clients' fears, frustrations, wants, and aspirations. Your services are highly sought after. They command higher revenue, and you are able to work with fewer clients.

This is because the quality and impact of your work are so significant that you get paid more, paid more often, and keep clients longer. You end up being able to step off the feast/famine rollercoaster and enjoy stability.

The opportunity to become wildly wealthy is within your grasp. At this stage, you are not a service provider, but a VITAL Advisor.

In summary, the journey from obscurity to VITAL involves a strategic narrowing of focus. You are moving from a generalist to a specialist. This journey is marked by a gradual shift. You begin by competing on price with a menu of services. You will move on to ad hoc advisory. Then you will reach the stage where you are competing on value and expertise with a productized transformational offer, which will lead to a position where you are not just valued, but considered vital by your clients.

Remember that VITAL stands for Valued, Impactful, Trusted, Agile, and Lucrative.

I don't know one accountant on this planet who wouldn't deep down want to be *VITAL* to their clients. A *VITAL Advisor* has all the luck:

- You attract the best opportunities.
- You hire the best staff.
- You get the best clients.
- You make the most money.
- You win all the awards.
- You have all the fun.

If you want to be VITAL, it is your job to make it happen.

CHAPTER 7
HOW TO FIRE TOXIC CLIENTS

We're going to talk about how to grow your practice by firing clients. This may seem counterintuitive, especially when I spend my time helping you get clients (rather than sacking them), but do stay with me on this one—It's super important!

Let's start at the beginning. Back when YOU started your business or your practice, you just wanted to work with anyone and everyone who could pay you.

When cash is tight, we often accept clients who are not always ideal. The ones who may not always be up to our standards, may not pay our full rates, or may not always be following the rules or boundaries that we have set in our own practice. Instead, we accept all sorts of behavior. This is because we need the cash.

This changes as your practice and client base grows. You start to realize that those are the people who we call *Vampire Clients*.

Vampire Clients pay just as much, or less than, all of your ideal clients, but they require more time and energy. They require your personal vibes, too.

They create havoc in both your life and your business. They may send you referrals, but never the good ones! They never get a great result from working with you because THEY are not ideal. As a result, *Vampire Clients* will rarely, if ever, give you testimonials.

As an act of self-love, you need to get these *Vampire Clients* out of your life!

When deciding whether or not a client is a vampire, keep in mind what defines an ideal client. They should make you feel good and give you energy-not suck it out of you!

When you think of all your clients answer these questions:

- Do I feel energized after working with that person?
- Do I look forward to working with them when I see them on my calendar or after speaking with them? Or do I feel drained?
- When I see them on my schedule, get an email from them, or hear a team member mention their name, does my heart sink?
- Do I say to myself, "Oh gosh, I can't believe I'm gonna have to talk to this person!"?

If you answer "yes" to these questions, it is a strong indicator that you have a *Vampire Client* on your hands. Here are two more questions to ask yourself:

- Would you want a practice full of that kind of client?
- Would you clone that client, and just work with people like that?

If the answer to both questions is a resounding "NO!", then what you've got on your hands is a non-ideal *Vampire Client*.

Many years ago I created a list of what constitutes a right-fit client for me and my business. It's a detailed list, but it has one overriding trait - they have got to be a nice person-kind and trustworthy.

I know from past experience that, if someone is not nice, and doesn't have the right character, they will eventually put a drain on both myself and my resources.

We are a loving company that really cares about our clients, so I am very careful about who I offer space in my world. You should be that way, as well. No amount of money is worth selling your soul to the devil.

Sometimes, it can be a bad match. They are not a bad person; they are just not your person. Not all people are for all people.

We're not ideal for chronic whiners and skeptics. This type of person makes excuses, doesn't do the work, and treats those around them (myself, my team, and other clients) in an unkind manner.

That's not somebody we want to play and work with. I spend a lot of time with my clients, so I want to feel good when I spend that time with them.

We're clear now, and everybody on the team is trained to look for red flags. We're very caring, and we don't let those people in. If we recognize that they're in, we make the decision that, maybe, it is time to say goodbye.

First and foremost, I want you to love yourself enough to get super clear on who's an ideal client and who isn't. This is because keeping a *Vampire Client* has consequences that you may not see at first.

Vampire Clients will suck the life out of you and the team, and eat into the profits of your business.

Joey, one of my new clients in the Business Advisor Academy, was recently sharing with me about how her team had gone through this. They had a really bad *Vampire Client*, that was not only making her exhausted and fed up but was affecting the team. Their happiness at work, and the quality of the work itself, was suffering.

After working with us for a few weeks, she got a new high-value advisory client (who was worth 102,000 dollars to her for a year's work). This high-value client brought her, along with her team, the energy, and confidence to sack an old *Vampire Client* of hers. Both her team and family were so happy!

I have to be honest with you. I still really struggle if I have a *Vampire Client*. You see, having a *Vampire Client* doesn't just affect me just when I am at work, or at that moment. It affects my overall mental and physical health. A *Vampire Client* keeps me awake at night; they become a topic of conversation with my husband at the dinner table or when traveling in the car; and it has even seen me snapping and shouting at the children, as I am so stressed out.

I reckon I am not alone in this. Many of my clients have confirmed they feel this way, too, with bad clients. Having one can really negatively change your life.

A *Vampire Client* can make your head hurt, your back ache, bring on depression, leave you unable to go to work, and lay you up in bed. It's pretty horrendous.

So why do we allow ourselves to keep *Vampire Clients* in our business? Why do we let them suck the life out of us?

Quite simply, it is because we are scared of saying no to money. *Vampire Clients* may be awful, but they pay the bills a lot of the time.

The ability to now market your accounting services means that there is no need to keep bad clients. Since the pool of clients is so much larger, you can just go and get a better one.

This always hasn't been the case, though. Before 1977, CPAs in America were not allowed to advertise. Here in the UK, the ICAEW didn't allow accountants to advertise their services in the public newspaper and other media until October 1, 1984.

Before this, accountants relied on word of mouth. Let's be honest-many still do! This means that getting rid of a *Vampire Client* is scary because they have no control over getting a new one.

We all know the saying, "A bird in the hand is worth two in the bush".

This old adage might be keeping you from making a very sensible decision. You are convinced that you are doing the right thing, so you can't let that bird fly away!

You are not sure where your next good client is coming from, and you are scared. So you keep the vampire client, and convince yourself this is the right thing to do both yourself and your staff. You need to pay the mortgage.

However, there is an answer, and the answer is one word—CONTROL.

You are allowed to advertise and get clients; you are no longer restricted and banned from advertising. Therefore, the thing you need to focus on is getting your practice to a point where you can get clients when you want to. You need to have a faucet of good leads that you can turn on and off at will. It all depends on whether or not you need (or want) a new client.

The definition of a *Vampire Client* will differ for individual firms and their owners. Different people can tolerate different stresses, so you have to come up with your own basic rules to follow.

Vampire Clients can show up in several ways, but there are sometimes when you just have to sack them—get them out of your company, and get them out of your life!

Here are some ideas to help you, and while these are created from MY values in life, I would be most surprised if you disagreed with me on them.

The first kind of *Vampire Client* is the one who is threatening you. This can be verbally, physically, or with court action.

The second *Vampire Client* that makes an appearance is one that is harassing you. It might be via email, on the phone, or sexually. What can be flattering at first may very well end up creeping you out. Without a doubt, this is most definitely a reason for dismissing a client!

No one should ever be creeped out, and it is your job to keep an eye out for clients who are doing this to your staff, too. It can go under the radar if your team is not prone to sharing. If that is the case, you need to check to make sure that the staff are ok.

It might take getting the question out in the open, so your staff feels comfortable sharing such issues.

Here is another one - if the client is lying to you. They are making up stories about why they could or couldn't do something, blaming your team when you know it's an untruth, or telling downright lies that you know are tales and not true. I have had a couple of clients do this to me. I knew that their claims were simply not true, and I had to quickly shut them out of the business.

How about the client who is making unreasonable demands? No amount of money should make you a doormat. If a high-value client is demanding too much from you, and it is affecting you mentally or physically, it is time to get the hell out of Dodge.

This next *Vampire Client* is slightly different, because the situation may be fixed, and you can avoid having to fire them. We have all run into a client that emails at unreasonable hours and expects immediate answers. It may be an onboarding problem.

If they were not made aware of your ground rules, and you didn't let them know you wouldn't be available to them 24/7, it is your responsibility to give them a chance to change their ways.

Put better boundaries in place, and see how it goes.

Here's another type of client that may not be under the *Vampire Client* heading—the ones that do not pay on time. I have a couple of clients that always pay me late. They need chasing every month, but they love my services, and I really like them. I let it go, but their late payments do cost me money. My team has to chase them, and it can get frustrating, but they are **not** *Vampire Clients*.

If they were, this would be the straw that broke the camel's back...

A good client is only good if they pay their bills. If they owe you money and don't pay their bills at all, send in the debt collectors and sack them.

You run a business, not a charity.

This next one is really important and rears its ugly head around tax season. They do not do as you ask, incur fines, and then blame you. This leaves you in a situation where they are angry at you when it's not even your fault. Arguments and horrible emails can follow. Voila! All those sleepless nights I mentioned earlier start to happen.

They start to play you off against other accountants.

Maybe the *Vampire Client* wasn't always one but is now becoming that way. If they play you off against the competition, then this is a big warning sign. Most of all, it means they are not seeing the value you provide, as they are being swayed by price or someone else's offering. If you cannot fix this problem, and articulate your value better than your competitor can, then you should let them go. Don't be held ransom.

Finally, letting go of this particular client is a no-brainer.

They are not sticking to the law. If you have a client who wants "creative" accounting, then sack them fast. You could end up in court. This could destroy your business, your marriage, and your relationships with everyone around you.

You are nothing without a good reputation. If you have a *Vampire Client* who holds you over a barrel and threatens to destroy your reputation, it is even more important to sack them.

In order to build your Freedom Practice, you need to get rid of *Vampire Clients* and fill your practice with high-quality clients. Advisory clients who value you and pay you what you're worth.

How exactly do you go about slaying a vampire? Here are some steps for you:

Step #1: Check Your Letter of Engagement. Can you sack them, or do you need to give notice?

Step #2: Finish Existing Projects. It's not good to leave in the middle of a project. Tie up all loose ends.

Step #3: Check your ego. This might sting a little, but it's important to check that this decision isn't about you and your bruised ego. Consider their behavior throughout your entire working relationship, and ensure this isn't just a one-off because you are in a bad mood.

Step #4: Put them on Probation. If a Vampire Client represents too large of a percentage of your revenue to let go right now, you might want to consider putting them on probation. Work on helping them become better clients.

Abraham Lincoln claimed that the best way to destroy your enemies is to make them your friends. In a similar vein, you can get rid of bad clients by turning them into good ones.

However, if the client fails, or outright refuses, to change their behavior within a given time frame, you will be well within your rights to end the relationship.

Step #5: Send a Letter of Disengagement. This should be short, polite, and emotionless. Don't gush or apologize. Explain to your client that your practice is moving in a new direction, and you will no longer be able to serve them in a way that is beneficial to them— not because you don't like working with them. No matter how much pain a client has caused you, you do not want to leave a relationship on bad terms or walk away with egg on your face.

The moment you decide to slay your *Vampire Clients* is the moment you will get freedom in your life. Watch your team relax that little bit more, your relationship with your partner and children improve, and your health come back to you.

On top of all of that, watch as you start to have fun running your practice again. A *Vampire Client* will suck the life out of you. Don't let that happen!

Your job is to slay the vampires fast and build a life of freedom...

CHAPTER 8
SIX ELEMENTS TO DESIGNING YOUR PERSONAL BRAND

Building a personal brand is extremely important. When I talk about creating an advisory practice and selling your advice, there is one thing that will really differentiate you in the marketplace—your personal brand.

This one thing is something that no one can copy. A tribe of raving fans will be created. Your impact in the marketplace will be catapulted above your competitors.
Let's dive in and explore what a personal brand is all about...

I am going to start this chapter with a very important saying, and that saying is, "You are who Google says you are". Back in 2015, Google said I was worth listening to. I was invited to speak at Google Campus and was asked to speak about building a personal brand. I have to admit, this is one of my proudest business moments. I had grown my brand to the point where Google thought my experience and my knowledge were good enough to share with their audience.

I remember the day well. I traveled up to the center of London from my Surrey home in the south of England, and I was so nervous! I was due to speak to a few hundred people, and it was kinda a big deal. This was my biggest and most prominent speaking gig to date. Public speaking has never been easy for me, and, as an introvert, it was way out of my comfort zone. So many people were going to be there, and I had no idea what was waiting for me. All I knew was that Google had this cool persona, and I was a 40-something, ex-corporate employee who was rather shy. There was nothing cool, hip, or trendy about me whatsoever! (Honestly, using this saying in itself is neither cool, hip, or trendy - I am sure my grown-up children will be mortified that I am putting this in my book!)

Anyway, I digress. I was so scared and nervous. The pit in my stomach was huge, due to the case of Imposter Syndrome I was suffering from.

As I arrived, there was a line of people out the door. The place itself was bright and airy, with a relaxed vibe. As I walked into the room, there it was-the stage! It was big, but not too big, and I started to relax. I turned my attention to those who were piling into the room to hear me speak, and I started the mantra I do before I walk on any stage.

I kept repeating to myself, "You are here to serve; You are here to serve".

I say this before I do any kind of marketing. The purpose of this particular mantra is to make sure I am being helpful to the people in the room, rather than having the focus on me. It is a reminder that whatever presentation I am giving isn't about me.

The constant repetition is another way for me to say to myself, "Don't focus on you Manda- what you look like or how people may judge you. This is about the people in the room. Help the people in the room, and you won't go wrong, Manda".

Then I was off! They introduced me, and I started my presentation. After 45 minutes, I had people clapping and giving me a standing ovation. I just stood there with my cheeks aglow and in a daze-I had done it! I had spoken at Google about how to build a personal brand.

It went down well. No one threw rotten eggs or moldy tomatoes! In fact, a line formed to speak to me after my talk. It was all highly successful!

My personal brand brought me an excellent opportunity. Ironically, it was to talk about that exact thing!

Fast forward to today, and I am going to share with you some of the information I shared with my audience.

Since 2015, there has been a slight shift in some of the actions you need to do, but the fundamentals are the same.

Here is my advice to help you build your personal brand, so you can sell your advice and build a business advisory practice that gives you a life of freedom.

A personal brand is essential. Whether you realize it or not, you already have one.

If I looked you up on Google, and I didn't find anything about you on the first page of the results, that's your brand. It's nothing.

If I found an out-of-date LinkedIn profile, or a bunch of random social media posts, that, too, is your brand.

People tend to think about a personal brand as bragging, self-promotion, and all about yourself.

It's actually something much more important—it's your reputation. It's how people perceive you—your friends, colleagues, or the general public.

In our connected world, every single one of us has a personal brand, whether we like it or not. It's what people say about you when you are not in the room with them. If they are saying nothing, then "nothing" is your personal brand.

This is because, whenever we engage with people, both in person and online, we're creating a reputational narrative about ourselves. Every online interaction, post, upload, or comment you place online adds to it.

Your reputation is already out there.

The question is, do you want to be the one who's driving and shaping the story, or do you want to chance it, and let the algorithms take control?

I think most people would agree that they want to take control, which means they need to make some very intentional decisions.

Remember, our brand stays in our hands and we are seen as we want to be seen...

Let me walk you through some steps to building a strong personal brand in a way that feels good.

I like to do this in two parts, with the first part being a brain dump.

You need to figure out what your goal is when it comes to your personal brand.

Let's start by answering a foundational question:

What do you want your personal brand to help you accomplish?

If you are reading this book, I can imagine your personal brand is going to be focused on wanting visibility, so you can sell your advice. Then again, maybe not. Don't let me put words into your mouth. As the term implies, it's your PERSONAL brand. It is personal to you, and your ideals. Not mine. So what do you want your personal brand to accomplish?

Are you looking to launch a new business or transition to a new industry?

Do you need your brand to reflect a new skill set that you want to be known for?

Right now, you may have a personal brand that screams accountant or tax expert. Is that what you want to be known for, and is that how you are going to make an impact in the world?

Maybe you're looking to make a bigger impact, and you work for one of the bigger firms. Maybe you want more responsibility or a promotion. Perhaps you need everyone to know all the amazing things that you've accomplished in your career, or maybe you're launching a new business and you want to build your brand around the products or services that you're offering. Whatever your goal is, write it down and make it specific. Doing so will ensure that you're working towards a clear outcome.

Next, you want to get clear on what you want to be known for.

In other words, how do you want people to describe you - start by answering the following question:

So what do you do?

I'm not just talking about your job title.

Are you an advisor who focuses on a money mindset, or do you help businesses grow and exit?

Maybe you're a really good project manager, who is reliable and always gets things done on time.

Maybe you're a creative that is really good at helping other people be more creative themselves; maybe you are great at systemizing; maybe you are a tech whiz; maybe it's not about selling your advice, but having a side hustle that you would like to be known for.

It could even be a passion that you would like to be known for.

What you want to do is dig deeper into the what, how, and why behind your work.

That way, it will be concrete and easy to remember. Just make sure to lead with something that doesn't cause confusion.

For example, I once coached someone who called herself an energy healer, which no one understood. When she started introducing herself as a fitness trainer who works with people who need to increase their energy. All of a sudden, everyone got it! It's about clarity, and being clear.

If you're stumped, think about how you can stand out from the crowd in your profession and industry.

What are the things that make you unique?

Are there specific talents and expertise that you've acquired in your career?

What do you know more about than most people? Sit down and make a list. You might start to surprise yourself with all the things you know.

This is where I talk about the 3 E's - Your education, your experience, and the essence of you. Remember, the essence of you is what makes it very personal, and it will be the backbone of your entire personal brand.

Your education may be that you are a qualified CPA; your experience might be that you have run a firm and grown it to multiple six figures, or have a team; maybe you have worked in the industry and helped another business grow and be really successful.

The essence of you is your personality. It is the bit that makes you shine. It could be your smile, your energy, your resilience, or your sense of humor. It could be that you are an introvert (this is certainly an essence of my personal brand).

So think about your education, your experience, and the essence of you....

Now, let's think about your audience. These are the people that you want to share your personal brand with. The reality is your personal brand is not just all about you. It's about the people you want to educate, give your advice to, and sell your advice to.

What advice do you want to give, or sell? Who are you looking at to sell, or give, your advice to? Who is a perfect fit for your education, experience, and personal essence?

Some marketers call it an industry niche. Others say it's a client persona. Whether you think of the person as someone in an industry or think of them through their personality type, you do need to be very, very clear on who they are, and make sure they are a great match for your personality.

What you can provide and who you provide it to are very important. So spend some time thinking about these two questions:

Who can most gain from what you have to share?

How exactly can you see yourself helping them?

This is the exciting bit; where it all starts to come together!

Now that you have brain-dumped all the answers, let's put them into something, which is known as the Personal Branding Pyramid. It is known for building excellent and clear client relationships.

The personal branding pyramid has six elements:

1. **Your Values**: What are your values? An example might be that you are honest and true to others.

2. **Your Personal Drivers**: Self-motivation and a positive attitude are highly desirable traits.

3. **Your Reputation:** Ask yourself what you are known for. If you are not known for anything yet, think about what you do want to be known for.

4. **Behaviors**: What do you want your personality to be seen as? Using myself as an example, I am known for being inspiring and an introvert. Do you think this happened by accident? No. I tell everyone I am an introvert, and I bring energy to my work so that I can inspire people. I tell

people I am an introvert so that other introverts look at what I do. It gives them the confidence that they can do it, too. On the surface, I don't look like an introvert because I focus on trying to inspire people. Therefore, I show up in spite of my shyness and fear.

5. **Your Skills:** An example might be that you are great at analyzing things, or seeing what others do not.

6. **Your Image:** What does your dress sense say about you? What is your style?

I want to share the power of the personal brand by using my friend, JJ the CPA, as an excellent example. Go check him out on YouTube.

At this moment in time, he is just shy of 100,000 subscribers. He is known for his great tax advice, but also his online image. He is confident, bold, and wears great three-piece suits. He originally became famous online for always holding a cigar, though the famous cigar isn't seen nowadays.

When we first connected, he reminded me of JR Ewing from the 80s show Dallas. Although, he is much more trustworthy than JR!

If you check him out on other social media channels, you will get to know about his wife - also named Amanda. He has a lot of love for both her and their children.

JJ's super strong personal brand has changed his business in only a few years. While I'm not saying you have to be that big and bold, turning up your personal brand from 1 to 10 will help you cut through the noise in the online world...

So there you have it - you are who Google says you are, and most of you are invisible right now.

If you google both your personal and business names, and your business name doesn't take up the first 3 pages of the search page, this is what you must aim for.

You can't show up on any social media platform, or have a personal brand website until you are clear on the 6 elements of the Personal Branding Pyramid.

Brain-dump all your ideas. Then answer the 6 questions I set out for you.

Follow up by getting that personal brand out into the world.

People buy people.

Show me who you are as a person, so that I can see if you are my people. Millions of people do what you do, but there is only ONE person just like you.

CHAPTER 9
5 WAYS TO SELL MORE ADVISORY SERVICES

I am going to share with you my top five strategies for selling your advisory/coaching offers, and what to do if your offers are currently being met with crickets.

This is something I'm so passionate about because it is a great way to give you a baseline of income. What's more, it is recurring. Most people will pay for advisory services for 12 months or more. If you get an advisory or coaching client, you could enjoy that higher revenue coming in for years to come.

It boosts your confidence and relieves anxiety when you know that you are growing your profits, and not just adding to your client roster. Additionally, it doesn't take a huge team to deliver the services.

There are many ways you can deliver your advisory/coaching offers. Some examples are providing clients with courses, memberships, and VIP days. However, the one I suggest you start with is a 1:1 coaching package. It is run initially for 3-12 months and is based on your signature methodology.

Now, this advice is different for some people.

If you already have a large number of advisory clients, then releasing a group program or mastermind class might be the logical next step.

If you only have one or two clients, then selling out your private 1:1 coaching/advisory offer is the thing that will give you more clarity, confidence, and take-home earnings.

I no longer do a ton of 1:1 coaching these days. I have maybe one or two coaching clients, and I charge them upward of £30k a year for my 1:1 coaching, as I teach you to do.

It's not something that I do often anymore because I like to free up some of my time for other things. However, if private advisory/coaching is how you want to be making the base of your income, that's awesome. That's something that a lot of my clients do really well. They either offer advisory only or add it to the compliance work they do for their clients.

Providing 1:1 advisory is amazing, as you get to add a lot of value to the people you work with. You will give them incredible transformations that will change both their businesses and their lives—maybe even their families and communities.

So that's why I love 1:1 private coaching.

If you want to learn how to sell out your private advisory coaching, keep reading.

The first tip that I have, when it comes to selling out your private coaching, is to design your advisory offer with your ideal client in mind. Start with the transformation first.

Many people will create programs, whether they are advisory offerings, or anything else, with the structure in the forefront of their minds. My clients will come to me and tell me that they want to hold a six-week online course, a three-month group program, or a one-year mastermind class.

They're choosing all sorts of programs with definitive time frames and will try to stuff the transformations they are offering into the tiny little boxes that they've created. What they need to do is shape the box to fit the result that the client wants. They have decided on the delivery mechanism first, instead of what is best for their clients.

I teach my clients to do something completely different. We create a signature methodology where they take their clients through 3 key milestones.

The first thing you want to start with is transformation.

If you're going to be selling private coaching/advisory packages, don't worry about the time frames you will be offering.

First things first: What's the transformation that your client will have working with you? What's point A to point B, and what do you want to have happen? What is point B, and what is the gap that you need to bridge for them to make their dreams and goals come true?

Here's the thing: You can have really big transformations, and you can have some smaller transformations, but they don't need to be the same offer.

For 80% of clients who are investing in your signature program, what is that transformation going to be?

What is it going to look like?

When I launched my first signature coaching package back in 2014/2015, the transformation that I had in mind was to have people escaping their corporate jobs, and making enough to cover their salary.

That was so they could confidently make the leap. In 6 months, we would build a brand new business that did 50-100k in revenue.

That was my goal, so that was the transformation I had in my mind.

Point A is where your client is struggling. They are in a job they do not enjoy, and want more freedom and their life back. Point B is where they will have monthly recurring revenue, the ability to escape the corporate world, and have developed a viable business. They are bringing in enough to give them options. Not any different to what I do now; helping accountants escape the compliance cage and create a freedom-based practice. What I do has never really changed.

The transformation for my clients, back in 2015, was saying goodbye to corporate and hello to a consistent income generated by their own business or self-employment.

The question I had to ask myself revolved around how my client would get to the point where they were generating enough money to escape their job. What would they need to learn and experience, and what did they need to have in place to get to that point?

I started by writing out a list of things like content, marketing, branding, messaging, offer, and hiring their first virtual assistant. I even worked with an accountant, who showed them how to set their business up from scratch, so it was set up in the right way.

I wrote about this signature methodology in the 5 steps I listed in my first book, *ESCAPE - the Definitive Guide to Escaping the Rat Race*.

This signature methodology accomplished two things. First, I had a framework for my marketing. Second, it gave my clients a clear framework for what we were working through together.

It never felt like they were just getting on a phone and asking me random questions for an hour a week. They actually had a process to follow, and they felt very safe knowing there was a method. They had control over what they needed to learn and put into action. Every step they had to go through was filled with intention and was leading them towards the transformation they wanted to achieve.

The structure that felt best for me was to have clients meet with me every other week for 50 minutes, and they would stay with me for six months. This included giving them email access. (By the way, I do NOT do this now. My private coaching clients have WhatsApp access—I do not have email in my life.)

They would email me. In return, I would assign them a to-do list, and they would share files with me, along with returning worksheets for me to check. That was the best possible structure for the transformation, knowing the process I had to take them through.

The first tip, when it comes to selling out your advisory offering, is to be able to understand why your offer is designed in the way that it is. Then go communicate that to your ideal clients; communicate that on sales calls; and communicate that in your marketing.

If people don't know what your advisory offer contains, or if they don't know why they need everything that's included, they're going to have questions and doubts. However, if you sell them on your process and your approach to advisory, you're going to sell them on the package. Be clear on what is going to be best for your ideal client. and not how long you think it should be, or you want it to be. Keep what the client needs in mind.

Focus on transformation, not transaction.

My second tip revolves around creating urgency with a launch strategy.

It is all about creating a sense of urgency by treating your advisory offering like a launch. Typically, in the advisory field, we don't have a specific offer for a specific client, so you must get your signature process in place. You have a secure offer to sell. The key is not to let this offer, or variations of your offer, become stagnant.

If potential clients believe they can sign up anytime for your advisory services, they may never do so. People often delay action if there's no sense of urgency.

Let me share with you this game-changing strategy: Treat your advisory offer as a launch. This approach introduces your advisory offering as a fresh, time-sensitive opportunity. I used this method in my early coaching days. For instance, I had a week where I heavily promoted my private coaching packages. The urgency of a limited-time offer, combined with the excitement of a launch, significantly boosted sign-ups and even led to a substantial cash influx.

During that week, I also conducted a seven-day livestream series on Facebook, tackling various client attraction topics.

This engaged a larger audience and generated a ton of visibility online, which introduced new people into my world. It nurtured those who were ready to buy and gave new people an insight into what I stood for.

Launch strategies are great, and the secret is not to get caught up in thinking you can only launch a specific offer once. It's about using different angles to launch the same thing multiple times in a year. As you get better at delivering your advisory offering, you will refine it further.

Refining your offer means that you will develop a new way to articulate it. When you have something new to say, or have something to say differently, you can launch again... and again.... and again!

Another tip is to launch your offering with different hooks. One launch could be the actual service offering. Another time, your launch could just involve getting calls booked in the diary. A live event you are holding where you fill the event and fill your advisory offering is yet another type of launch. It takes a little bit of thinking about the launch model, but it can be very viable and very rewarding. You are making a big impact when you are in launch mode.

It is now time to cover my third tip, which is all about the one-time session upsell.

The one-time session upsell is a very powerful way to demonstrate how great you are while giving the client a quick win. It could be one of a whole host of options. You may offer a 2-hour planning session, or maybe a profit-boosting power session. (It could even be a Xero training session.)

Using one of these sessions as a jumping board, you can sell people into your long-term advisory.

Let's say you have a 12-month program priced at $2,500 a month, which would be $30,000 for the year. You could offer a half-day goal-setting or planning session for $1500. Then, at the end of the session, ask your client about their experience and takeaways. This is a good way to introduce your longer-term program, where you credit the cost of the planning session to the total price.

This approach is psychologically compelling. Clients feel they're getting a deal since they're "saving" the cost of the initial session. It's a powerful sales technique that I've leveraged multiple times. Even during my launch phases, I offered these bite-sized sessions, which effectively led to more extensive commitments.

In summary, remember, the key to selling out your advisory services lies in creating urgency and smartly utilizing initial, lower-cost sessions to lead to more comprehensive packages. By using these strategies, you're not just offering a service; you're providing an experience that clients are eager to embark on.

Remember, the goal is transformation and results. A client who experiences your expertise in a shorter session will be more inclined to imagine the possibilities of a longer commitment.

We are now on to the fourth tip, which is all about getting comfortable with the sale.

Becoming comfortable with the sales process is a common hurdle I've noticed, especially with my new clients. It is the discomfort they have when asking for the sale. If you're able to get potential clients on a discovery call, but struggle to close them, it's often due to a lack of confidence in this area.

Here, we need to reframe sales as a whole. If you transform your perspective on sales, you can transform your profits. Some of you might be tempted here to say,

"Ohhh, Amanda, everyone I speak to buys from me!"

That leads me to think that you probably have a pricing problem. We don't want everyone to buy; we want the right people to buy.

We may avoid sales by undercharging because we are uncomfortable with sales. We make it easy for our clients and ourselves. Being uncomfortable with sales shows up in many ways.

Here is the solution: Rather than seeing it as a pushy or unpleasant task, view it as an opportunity to serve. Focus on understanding the client's pain points, and how your services can facilitate their journey from point A to point B. Bring a mindset of service and help to the conversation, and you'll find asking for the sale becomes much more natural and effective.

Additionally, don't rush the sale. After presenting your offer, pause and allow the client time to consider. This space is crucial, and it can significantly impact the outcome of your sales efforts.

Sales are about helping.

Movies, such as The Wolf of Wall Street, have conditioned us to think that sales are slimy, and not about helping people. This could not be more wrong!

Sales are all about helping people. There are people out there right now, desperate for help! If you do not sell to them, they could lose everything.

Selling is serving, and with that reframe, you will sell a lot more in the right way.

Let's bring this chapter home, and move on to tip five. This is one which most people forget; the fortune is in the follow-up.

Rather than constantly casting a wide net indiscriminately regarding your offerings, focus on warm leads. These are individuals who have already interacted with your content or your accounting services. Your compliance clients could be warm leads.

I find it very interesting when accountants tell me that their clients are not ideal for advisory services. They assume that compliance clients can't afford them, or will not pay them. This assumption is often wrong. If you do not offer them help, they cannot say yes or no. Your job is to offer better help to current clients. If they refuse, then that is their choice, but you must offer it to them.

Nothing will annoy you more, than if you do not offer, and you find out that they have dropped 50k on business coaching for the year. Your clients are warm leads, and you need to offer them more services!

Going back to those who haven't yet bought from you, you can keep track of these leads, perhaps in a simple Google sheet, and regularly reach out to them. This can drastically improve your conversion rates.

Remember, it often takes multiple touchpoints before someone is ready to invest in your services. By nurturing these warm leads, you're not only increasing your chances of a sale, but you're building a more personal and meaningful connection with potential clients.

There you have it—the 5 ways to sell your advisory services.

Let's recap:

1. Design your offer with the transformation in mind first.
2. Create urgency with a launch strategy.
3. Provide one-time session upsells.
4. Get comfortable with the sale.
5. Follow up with warm leads.

I leave you today with one final thought.

Always keep in mind that your work is a service to the world, and getting paid for it is a fair and necessary exchange.

With these tools and mindsets, you're well-equipped to make a significant impact as a business advisor.

CHAPTER 10
CONQUERING IMPOSTOR SYNDROME ON YOUR ADVISORY JOURNEY

In this chapter, I am diving into something very personal that will have probably affected you at one time or another in your life—Impostor Syndrome.

Have you ever asked yourself these questions?

- Am I really good enough to give people advice?
- Do I have the knowledge?

Have you ever thought to yourself:

- "I have never run a large business myself, nor have I ever sold a business before."
- "I am just out in the advisory business, and I have never run an accounting firm before—I am not fully qualified".

These are just a few ways the dreaded impostor syndrome shows up in people's lives.

You are constantly telling yourself, "I am not good enough, I am not good enough..."

A lot of us struggle with impostor syndrome, and I still struggle with it to this day.

What I do know is that sharing your experience and education is one of the scariest things one can ever do.

It's like poking your head above the parapet; waiting for someone to shoot it off.

What I would love to achieve through this chapter is to get clear on what impostor syndrome means, so that you can actively confront it.

Webster's dictionary defines impostor syndrome as a psychological condition characterized by persistent doubt in one's abilities or accomplishments, accompanied by the fear of being exposed as a fraud, despite the evidence of one's ongoing success. Did that hit home? Quite possibly...

The two phrases that I thought were really interesting were 'persistent doubt' and 'despite the evidence of one's ongoing success'.

I joined the profession officially in 2016. Up until then, I had only ever experienced what it was like to be the daughter of someone who ran a tax firm. I had never been an accountant, or run an accounting firm myself.

In 2016, my father, a tax technician, asked me to help the profession with marketing. While I had never helped an accountant before, I had helped hundreds of clients in my business get really good at marketing and growing their businesses.

Plus, I had been a director of a very large corporate events business for many years before setting up my own business. I had worked with huge marketing budgets, and I had personally built my own business to multiple six figures before moving into the accounting profession.

When my dad asked me to help accountants, it was a weird feeling. Doubt kicked in, despite all the success I had in the corporate world. How could I help a profession I knew so little about?

I spent nearly a year doing a deep dive into the profession, learning all I could. This involved reaching out to institutions, accounting bodies, my peers, and the accounting industry in general.

Everyone loved the ideas I brought to the table, but the self-doubt continued. Despite being talented and having something accountants needed, I felt like an impostor.

Looking back to 2016, my dad's opinion of me was what gave me the gumption to think that I was even capable of becoming an advisor to the accounting profession. A slightly older than middle-aged white male in a traditional grey suit (Sorry, Dad!) thought I had just what you all needed. That planted a small voice inside me that kept saying, "Why not? Why not you? It could be fun- just give it a try"

Now, what made that little voice even louder was a burning desire inside of me to help and change people's lives. I had seen what the profession had done to my father: heart surgery, stress, and depression. I knew that I could help and change this situation, so others could be spared what he went through.

On top of that, I knew what my life was like as a child of someone who ran a tax firm, and used to be employed by one of the Big Four, in London. During the summer, Dad was physically present, but the stress caused him to be unhappy and grumpy. He was incapable of being present for me at the emotional level.

I remember the Christmas holidays when Dad would sneak off to his upstairs office in our house because he had work to do. (Tax season is the end of January in the UK.)

When I was fifteen, Dad managed to squeeze in a four-day vacation to France for the family. I made him so mad that he made us leave early and come back home.
All of this happened because the profession just isn't conducive to a work-life balance.

These memories and situations are what I use to fuel me. The truth in me knew that I had to do as my dad had asked. I had to show up and help the profession get better clients, and run a better practice.

It started with one client, but I was steadily gaining from there. I had 30 clients in total, but then Covid hit the world and catapulted me into the thick of it! Over 300 clients and 18 months later, I was well and truly ingrained in the accounting profession. I am probably never likely to leave.

I had to do the work because people needed me.

I use the term 'gumption' a lot; I believe it comes before confidence. I first heard the term from the actress Hayley Mills. I think it was in her movie Pollyanna, but it might have been the original 60s movie, The Parent Trap.

Gumption means doing something with guts, which is really hard when impostor syndrome kicks in.

However, the word 'gumption' has propelled me forward when my feet seem glued to the floor and I cannot move. There is a well-known book on this subject. It is Feel the Fear and Do It Anyway, by Susan Jeffers. She talks about taking negative thinking (which can show up in one form or another, including impostor syndrome), and reintroducing your mind into positive thought patterns.

That is the solution to moving you through impostor syndrome.

What I have continuously done to move through stages of impostor syndrome is to have the gumption to move forward, even when I feel I am not worthy or able. I have to look it straight in the eye and take the first step. This is how I move forward— I continuously take first steps every day. The cure for impostor syndrome isn't some magic knowledge that I can get, but in fact, the way to free myself from the impostor cage is to show up in life courageously. That is the point. If I do not take any risks, I cannot create any magic.

Sharing your education and experience in the world is one of the most vulnerable things you can do, but that is what makes it so exciting.

The ability to share your insights, and expertise, and HELP people; this is where the magic happens. You will be helping people and creating that bigger impact.

Sharing my advice has been the gateway to allowing me to build my own courage, day in and day out. When I stare at a blank piece of paper or start to map out this podcast, for example, the possibilities are endless. I do not undervalue the fact that you are reading this chapter and have me speaking in your mind. Every word I say, every sentence I speak, and every message I share has to be of value; otherwise, I am just wasting your time, and time is the one thing you cannot get more of.

I totally get how imposter syndrome shows up because I had to have the courage to write this book so that I could help you. As I sit and write each chapter, a narrative in my mind is going around saying, "Who am I to share this with you?"

Some may say, "Don't be daft, Amanda," but it can be intimidating and paralyzing. I ask myself, "Will people like it? Will they want to work with me, or will they read the first chapter and put the book down?"

Everything crosses my mind. Even before I hold calls with my clients, I get nervous.

These people have invested in getting my help. Despite thousands of hours of making videos and holding coaching sessions behind me, I still worry I am not good enough.

Here is the thing: I tap into gumption and courage. That being said, you need to understand that courage and gumption don't start in the mind; they start in movement.

As Elizabeth Gilbert says, "I don't sit around waiting for passion to strike me. I keep working steadily because I believe it is our privilege as humans to keep making things".

You just have to start. When I started to create, it helped me break free from impostor syndrome and allowed me to share my gifts with the world.

Life continues to amaze me, and it continues to remind me that on the other side of the facade of fear, there is a field full of every single one of your desires. When you allow yourself to push through and break the chains in your mind, your mind will be blown away daily, and gratitude will start to overflow.

I'm invited to speak to accountants who run businesses I have never even worked in. By owning my identity as an advisor, I've had the privilege of sharing my work with huge software companies, and am asked to go on stage as a keynote speaker.

I have been an advisor to partners in accounting firms that have a revenue of over 7 million a year, and I have had the privilege to help new sole practitioners launch a business and escape the Big Four.

The one thing that I'm most humbled by is having built a community of supporters. I call them my 'tribe'. I call YOU my "tribe". You continue to affirm what I do by reminding me how my advice has inspired you to show up, share, and express your views and ideas in ways that I never thought possible.

Having a tribe starts a ripple effect for every person, place, and thing in your life. Sharing my advice, life experiences, and thought leadership has enabled me to have the joy and happiness I needed. The funny thing is, the more I share, the less stress I feel.

I am currently recording fewer videos at the moment, which would normally send me into a pit of depression, as I would not be sharing my gift, but I have taken the time to invest in creating both a podcast and this book. I am still creating but in a different way.

Helping people is the giver of joy, even for those who are not creative! Focus on giving value and watch your joy soar.

I'm telling you about my own experiences, but you're not just watching from the outside. You're also a creator, who is playing an important part in this big, connected world.

I've seen a lot of skilled people, including myself, held back by impostor syndrome. Feeling like they're not good enough stops them from moving forward. The way to overcome this is through being creative and brave.

It's not just about being creative; it's about sharing your creativity with others. When we all share our ideas, we mix them together and come up with even better ones.

This is how we become stronger.

Combining our ideas allows us to create new solutions and innovations for the world.

Have you ever read the book, *The Top Five Regrets of the Dying: A Life Transformed*, written by Bronnie Ware?

These five regrets are:

1. I wish I had the courage to live a life true to myself, not one others expected of me.
2. I wish I hadn't worked so hard.
3. I wish I had the courage to express my feelings.
4. I wish I had stayed in touch with my friends.
5. I wish I had let myself be happier.

I thought it was interesting that, out of those five regrets, two included courage.

I work in a profession that, 10 years ago, was still extremely male-dominated. That is changing. Slowly, but surely, we are seeing more women of all ages start to make a difference.

When I went to my first Accountex exhibition here in the UK in 2017, I remember looking around the room at so many men standing on stage and saying their bit. Again, impostor syndrome kicked in. Instead of being a hindrance, it provided the fuel to make a difference and give us women a voice, too.

Different things fuel different people. What I do know is that whether you are male, female, or identify as neither or both, it's not about that. These thoughts can hold you back, but you have to have the courage to step out of your comfort zone.

Less than 10 years after walking into a male-dominated accounting profession, I am seeing these males (whom I once felt inferior to) leave the profession slowly but surely. They are now retiring, and bowing out of a world they perceive they cannot keep up with.

I felt like I was taking a risk when I joined the profession, but to live a life that's true to you, this is what you have to do. This is exactly what sharing our thoughts with the world requires of us. We have to show up bold, courageous, and vulnerable. We have to have gumption where confidence eludes us.

Even when you are shaking in the midst of sharing your advice and thoughts; even if you are standing on the stage or presenting to a crowd, this is what you have to do.

Go to the stage to change the world. We need people who want to bring more value than ever before.

We need accountants, tax technicians, business advisors, lawyers, and teachers who can be the leading edge of imagination. I would argue that you have more knowledge about the economy and business growth than the business coaches who get paid thousands of dollars with little to no experience or financial insights.

Maybe you haven't permitted yourself to express that aspect of yourself, but I can tell you this now: with gumption and knowledge, you can let go of impostor syndrome. You won't regret it.

CHAPTER 11
THE SECRET TO BUILDING AN AUDIENCE FAST

In this chapter, I am going to do a deep dive into one of the most powerful, if not THE most powerful, ways to build an audience of ideal clients that feel some kind of trust towards you–fast!

Quickly building an audience is a highly underutilized concept; however, when implemented, it capitalizes on the word "leveraging" - leveraging time, effort, and results.

The biggest problem that most people have when they embark on selling a high-value offer is that they are little known—they haven't got an audience that knows about them. Therefore, they struggle to get clients.

There is a solution that capitalizes on the effort, investment, credibility, and trust that others have built with your target market. It is about aligning yourself with non-competitive businesses and people who can short-cut your timeline to success. They can give you a surge in awareness by introducing your products and services to their audience on a collaborative basis. It can be a win-win for both parties.

As I have mentioned, it is the most powerful strategy available, and unlike organic content marketing (posting on LinkedIn or Instagram, etc.), you are not at the mercy of the algorithm.

Additionally, unlike paid advertising, you are not at the mercy of giving all your money to Zuckerberg.

There's no such thing as a self-made person. Building a successful practice is a team sport. The spirit of partnership is not about the legal definition; it's not about written contracts.

It is about understanding that:

- Whoever you want to reach, someone already knows them.
- Whenever you want to be seen as credible, someone can endorse you.
- Whenever you need someone to help, someone can.

Many different kinds of partnerships and strategic alliances include:

- Partners that give you helpful recommendations.
- Referral partners that send clients your way.

- Introducers to the team or software you might need.
- Affiliates that promote your offer and get a commission.
- Joint ventures where you team up with someone and do something together.
- A strategic alliance where you align yourself with someone to benefit both of you.
- Legal partnership - which is self-explanatory.

From these kinds of partnerships, the Joint Venture/Strategic Alliance partnership is the one that I really want to focus on.

Let me give you an example of a strategic alliance that I first did when I came into the accounting profession. You see, my problem was that I was not known in the profession; when I first joined in 2016, I did not have one accounting connection on my LinkedIn or one accountant on my Facebook. My audience consisted of people who wanted to escape their day job and start a consulting/coaching business - none of whom were accountants.

I had to look at my time, financial resources, and situation very seriously.

If I wanted to get in front of accountants, what was the best way to do this?

Was it to start creating content and hope that accountants would connect with me?

Yes, I did need to do that; I needed to create content to show my expertise and experience and position myself as someone who knew what they were talking about. This strategy alone would have been slow; it takes time to gain an audience through content creation alone.

Did I need to do Facebook advertising? Well, no - I had yet to understand my ideal client enough, or have a lead magnet that I knew people wanted, so using Facebook Advertising would have been a gamble, and I could have lost a lot of money.

I was left with one strategy that I knew worked exceptionally well. If I coupled it with organic marketing, it would catapult me in front of my ideal target market. Additionally, it would give me instant credibility.

I knew that the way to start building my audience in droves was to tap into joint venture partnerships and strategic alliances.

I am sure you have heard of Ignition App. Well, back in 2016, they were known as Practice Ignition.

Practice Ignition, or Ignition as they are now known, had just what I needed—accountants and bookkeepers using their product and a large community online that I could get in front of.

I had something that they didn't have at the time...

This was expert knowledge around marketing and sales. Maria Lauring, who was in charge of customer success at Practice Ignition, and I decided to team up and bring a series of webinars to her audience. These webinars were designed around how to use social media to get clients.

This was a really good partnership because between us we had three things, which every good JV partnership should have:

- Strong Brand
- Expertise
- Audience

Now, for an ideal partnership to happen, each party needs to have at least two of these three.

I brought the expertise to the Ignition partnership; I had been posting content online for many years and had a strong brand, albeit not yet within the accounting profession.

Ignition, on the other hand, had a strong brand in the accounting profession and the audience I needed. So, this partnership was a perfect fit for both of us. I brought the expertise of sales and marketing, and they brought the audience.

It was great - so great that over three years, I not only ran numerous webinars for them but also sponsored their pre-show events in London.

I teamed up with both them and the Association of Chartered Certified Accountants in 2019 for a week-long roadshow. This alliance alone enabled me to build my email database by thousands and showcased me as the go-to marketing consultant for the accounting profession here in the UK. I can attribute thousands of pounds of revenue to this strategic alliance alone; never mind the other alliances and partnerships that were formed off the back of this one.

Accountex, the leading exhibition here in the UK for accountants and bookkeepers, was another partnership that I had. I approached Zoe Lacy-Cooper, the Event Director at the time, and asked her if she would be interested in supporting me in launching the BAMAs - a hair-brained idea of mine where we celebrated accounting firms that were great at marketing. The BAMAs stood for British Accounting Marketing Awards.

Zoe said yes! She, and several other key people from the accounting profession, were judges. We had five awards with five judges for each award. These awards enabled me to reach out to people in the profession and build great relationships with them, by asking them to be judges.

I had the expertise; these guys had the audience and brand. Can you see the pattern here? This is why partnerships are so powerful, especially when you need to reach a large audience.

In a way, we are also in partnership with social media platforms. These social media platforms have our audience, and if you post on them, you can showcase your expertise and build your brand. Joint ventures and partnerships are all about one thing - LEVERAGE - moving you faster along your journey by leveraging other people's contacts or brands. The benefits of such partnerships are manifold.

Here are some advantages of leveraging:

- Shared resources and expertise
- Increased credibility
- Cost-effective marketing
- Cross-promotion
- Diversification of content
- Referrals
- Pooling data and insights
- Increased media engagement
- Enhanced-value propositions

I hope by now that I have shown you the power of a strategic alliance or partnership. What I would like to do next is dive into a few tactics that you could use to get started.

First off, please remember that a partnership must be a combination of three things, and you need two of them:

- A strong brand
- Expertise
- An audience

You might be tempted to dive into trying to find yourself a partner who has a big audience right from the moment you launch your business or practice, but I would warn you to stand down and make sure you have built up two or three elements.

When building a strong brand, you need to have a firm vision of what makes an ideal client, a clear brand message, and be visible in the media. This could be online and/or offline. Additionally, you may need a strong local presence if you are looking to build your business in your area.

To be seen as an expert, you need to have content showcasing your expertise, credible awards, or relevant exams that you have passed; Show everyone that you have been in the field for some time and have case studies of results, for example.

Don't overthink this section. You can be an expert by being a qualified accountant, or having worked as an accountant or CFO for a few years already in industry. The audience one is self-explanatory.

Some seven years after building my brand, my expertise, and my audience in the accounting industry, I have all three to bring to the table when it comes to joint ventures.

Whichever of the three strategies you are missing, you can build up. It just takes time.

Assuming you have the expertise and brand, and have been showing up online and in media for a while, we can now start to think about who might be a good strategic alliance/partnership for you. The best way to find these people is to network online and offline. When talking with my clients, we create a hot list of the top 10 partnerships that could be a great fit.

You can have a look at marketing agencies that might target your ideal client; you bring the financial coaching, and they help businesses grow with marketing, as an example. You can have a look at publications, exhibitions, conferences, and chambers of commerce; you can reach out to software companies directly. There are so many options. My favorite way of finding partnerships is to look at exhibitions that have my audience. I look at who is exhibiting there and reach out to those businesses, as you both want to reach the same audience.

Right now, I feel I might just be throwing loads of ideas at you, but please remember, this is not a difficult strategy. You need to find someone that has your audience and reach out to them.

You then need to get a quick call in the diary to see if there is anything that you could do together. Don't be scared about reaching out to people. This is an easy conversation. You are not selling or asking anything of anyone. You are just having a conversation.

I am going to give you a couple of scripts you could use - one is for strangers and one is for friends.

Let's dive in with the one for strangers first. Just send a message on social media/email and get a call in the diary to see if there is a win/win opportunity.

Strangers:

Hi (First name)

You and I haven't met yet - but we both work with (insert niche) and are non-competitive.

I've heard good things about you. I'd love to catch up and see if there is any way we can help each other out. It'd be great to get to know you, and see how I can help.

Would you be open to that?

Amanda

Friends:

Hey (First name)

Hope you are well... It's been a while...

I'd love to catch up with you to hear the latest and see if there is any way we can help each other out.

Would you be up for that?

Amanda

Let's dive back into the process. When you create a partnership, what kind of thing could you do together?

As a starter, sharing a webinar with their audience, and having them do the same, is a nice win-win for both parties. Teaming up and running an event together could be another win-win. You could even consider writing a whitepaper together.

Another option would be if you could start small and write a blog for their website; they could do the same for you.

Start with a conversation. If you have the same ideal clients, if your values align and you like them, and if you like their business and they like yours, there are only upsides to this approach.

Through such collaborations, you can significantly expand your audience, credibility, and ultimately, your success.

CHAPTER 12
HOW I STRUCTURE MY TIME IN MY PRACTICE

Let me share how I structure my hours, days, weeks, and months so that you can also optimize your time management to fit in with YOUR goals and dreams.

The biggest struggle when you start or grow a business is finding time, and finding that somewhat elusive balance between work and life. This can be especially hard if you have other responsibilities outside of work and are a primary caregiver for children, parents, or other family and friends.

It can feel like a never-ending struggle to find time for yourself - time to breathe and recoup your energy. It can feel like you are always "on"; you must be doing something wrong because you feel overwhelmed with your huge to-do list.

I know because this is how I used to be, especially when the children were young. You might not know about my past, and how I came to run my own businesses, so I will let you have a bit of the backstory right now. It is relevant to what we are covering today.

There is a saying that time is a great equalizer - it is the only thing you cannot get more of; it is finite.

Finding time is hard when you are the one responsible for everything and everyone. You too often wear all the hats and do all the things.

I have been in the advisory game for 15 years and have shown up as a consultant and agency owner since my youngest child, Annabelle, was 4 years old.

When my children were just 4 and 7, I decided that I needed to start my own business. I was a single mum and sadly had got myself into a bit of a pickle with a bad relationship and was on housing benefit (housing assistance for my US readers). I was disappointed in getting myself into this position and knew that I had to get off assistance as fast as I could.

Here's the thing: In my past corporate life, I was an Event Director. I was responsible for a small team and running exhibitions all around the world. It involved me acting as a marketer, a salesperson, and a manager.

I was also an innovator. I had to go around the world and look at whether there were events that were suitable for buying for the business I was working for.

When I was living on a housing benefit, at 35 years old, I was too far from London to go back into the corporate world, and I was far too responsible for my children as their full-time caregiver.

I made the decision to start my own business, in the hope that I would be able to make enough income while my children were at school, so I could get off assistance.
There are a lot of things I can share about this journey. I could go into how I had to learn new things like social media and digital marketing, how I had to get outside of my comfort zone and start networking, or how I set up a copywriting business and never moved past £25 an hour (until I got a mentor that showed me a better way of doing things).

However, that is not what we are covering here. This chapter is all about how, over the past 15 years, I have run my diary in a way that has enabled me to grow to an agency with 1.5 million pounds in revenue. I will show you how I went from a single mum, who was able to still do the school run. through to today as a woman with adult children and a life of freedom.

Now that you know the backstory, I am going to share with you how I managed my time as I went from a

Dream Up (where I had the idea of running my own business), to having a Freedom Practice.

The stages I have gone through are:

1. **Dream-Up** - I had the idea of starting my own business.
2. **Start-Up** - I took the idea to the world and got a couple of clients.
3. **Grow-Up** - I dramatically grew my client base, my team, and my revenue to 1.5 million.
4. **Scale-Up** - I sorted out my business model, scaled my time without sacrificing my income, and created what I now call a Freedom Practice.

When I was in the Dream-Up stage, I had no money, but I had a lot of time. As I sat drinking my Diet Coke in the sun in my back garden, I mapped out what I thought might be a good idea. I started to think that I could set myself up as a copywriter and write copy for newsletters, magazines, and businesses that wanted to have press releases written, etc.

I didn't have any direct experience in this, but I knew that I could write; I could write fast.

Additionally, I had my mother's help. She was great at proofreading, so I knew that if I could get the clients, she could help me hone my skills. My dream was to get a few clients and work around the children.

This Dream-Up stage was about 6 months long. I started talking to people about my idea, and this is when people showed their true colors. Some supported me, but some of my friends were upset that I was going to be busy and not be around for the mothers' meetings and tea and cake natters. Sadly, most of the naysayers are no longer in my life, and I learned the lesson that not everyone will support you very early on.

This Dream-Up stage was all about conversations and research. I looked at who was doing something similar to what I wanted to do, bought myself a computer, and put content into a Word document with all of my ideas. It was a very exciting stage. My life consisted of getting the children out of bed in the morning, making them breakfast, and then working on my ideas. When they were at school, I would knuckle down. I stopped when they came home from school and started again the next day.

The children also went to their dad's every other weekend, so I built a lot of the foundations on the weekend. When my friends were out drinking and enjoying themselves, I sat in my front room, scouring the internet and reading business books.

Once I was sure that copywriting was going to be my thing, I moved into Start-Up mode. This mode was exhausting. Even when I had a corporate job with loads of pressure and a team, I didn't work as hard as when I was in Start-Up mode.

This is where I went from no revenue to 100k revenue. This start-up mode lasted about 5 years, and my income fluctuated from £25 an hour through to the latter years, where I changed my business model from copywriting to being a social media trainer, and then marketing consultant.

Getting from no revenue to 100k was about sacrificing my time. I would take the children to school at 8:15 a.m. every morning, so I would wake up at 6 a.m., and start marketing from 6:30 to 7:30 a.m. I would write blogs and social media content while the world slept.

I would then take the children to school and work through until school pickup time. Then I would stop working again to play mum. I had a strict bedtime routine, so the kiddies were in bed by 7:30 p.m. every night; this was when I went back to work, and I would work through to 2 a.m. some nights. On the weekend, the children would either be with me, and I would spend the days with them, or they would be with their father. When they were with him, I would work.

If you have ever heard the term 'hustle' used, this is what I did. Every moment of every day was hustling. I gave up going out; I didn't see my friends very often. When I did see them, I certainly didn't let my hair down and drink, as I had to be 100% switched on the next day to squeeze in some work. If I had five minutes, I did something; there was no time for lollygagging!

At the time, I didn't realize that I was doing what most people don't do when they start a business. I went all in and gave up everything, apart from being a full-time mum. I managed to juggle that and being a start-up, but friends, drinking, and partying had to go. Not that partying was something I enjoyed that much anyway; I am a bit of an introvert.

To this day, I think one of the reasons I became successful was because I was at rock bottom. Being on housing benefit meant that I knew what the worst life could look like, and I didn't want to stay there. So I did what most people wouldn't do—I didn't permit myself to have a break. I didn't say I deserved to go out, because I had no money and couldn't give the children the future they wanted. I had to choose my hard. Did I want my hard to be working hard, or did I want my hard to be no money? I chose to work hard. (FYI: The average wage in the UK is just shy of £36,000 a year, and I was making £100,000.)

When I was in Start-Up mode, the first thing I did every day was marketing. The last thing I did every day was marketing. When the children were at school, I was networking face to face. My weekends were spent learning and marketing. No one was coming to save me, so I had to do the work myself.

Once I had gotten to the stage where I was no longer needing help from the government, I moved into the Grow-Up stage. I had clients, but I did not have to get up at 6 a.m. or work till 2 a.m. anymore. There was a shift, so my day had to change. Most people I work with tend to be in the Grow-Up stage. They already have a few clients, so they are in the weeds doing the work; they now find juggling time more difficult than when in the Start-Up Stage.

In the Start-Up Stage, you often have excitement and the thought of possibilities to fuel you.

In the Grow-Up Stage, you can often find you are exhausted and begging for breathing space.

You need to run your day differently. You might have a team, or you might be working with clients 5 days a week, and this is where you must introduce something I call *Time Mapping*.

I learned *Tiime Mapping* from my first marketing coach, a guy called Rob Scott, who was a super cool guy that I reached out to when I was shifting from start-up to grow-up. He taught me how to schedule my days so that I had time for everything.

The first thing you have to do when you time map is work out everything you do in a day. The best way to do this is to spend two weeks jotting down what you're working on every 30 minutes.

This means that, at the end of every day, you will have 24 or more half-hour segments that document all the work you did. Each segment might include client work, emails, marketing, talking to your friends, traveling, taking children to school, doing homework, or watching Netflix. This includes the whole lot; write down what you do all day, not just during work hours.

Time Mapping is how you look for leaks of time, along with what activities can be grouped together.

I have a process called *CDS* for this, and my clients use it to see what they can **C**ut, **D**elegate, or **S**ystemize—hence *CDS*. The process of Cutting, Delegating, and Systemizing enables us to get a clear picture of what you really should be working on. At the Grow-Up Stage, you need to move yourself into a position of marketer, salesperson, and probably advisor/coach. Try and remove everything else from your plate.

Once you have worked out what you need to fit in a day, you need to schedule it. The way I recommend scheduling everything is to pick focus days.

When I was in the Grow-Up Stage, my days looked like this:

- Monday - Marketing
- Tuesday - Client Day
- Wednesday - Sales
- Thursday - Client Day
- Friday - Relationship Building - so still marketing, but this could involve face-to-face meetings and networking.

On top of this, I scheduled time every day to do three things.

First, I created a social media update as soon as I got back from the school run.

Second, while getting around for the day, I would listen to podcasts and books to inspire me and give me ideas to talk about in either my video or my social media article.

Third, I would reach out to 20 people a day on social media, add them to my platforms, and start a conversation with them. This would take me about 90 minutes.

This meant I was spending the first two hours of every day working ON my business, not IN my business. This is the biggest struggle that people have when they are trying to grow. They are stuck in the weeds, so they can't grow the business. This is why you have to do the CDS Process and get everything off your plate.

In growth mode, I was still working hard, but I wasn't starting my day at 6 a.m. Instead, it was starting at 7 a.m., listening to and consuming ideas as I was getting the children ready for school.

Once I got the children from school in the afternoon, I would leave them to their own devices; I would go back to work until about 5:30 p.m. Then I would make dinner while they pottered around me, and we talked.

During the Grow-Up Stage, I would still work weekends when the children were not around, and I would work some evenings if I was inspired. My life had changed by this point, and I was remarried, so I had a little more help in the evenings.

Let's recap the Grow-Up Stage. I spent two hours doing marketing every day, without missing a day. Monday and Friday were exclusively for marketing; Wednesday was for sales calls; Tuesdays and Thursdays were client days. I ran my diary like this for a few years, and it worked wonders. I went from 100k a year to having 100k months.

This moves me on to how I scaled my business, but not in a way that you might imagine. At this point in my business life, I was 10 years in; I was tired; I had a business with a big team and a lot of responsibility. My children were growing up, and I wanted more freedom in my life.

My Scale-Up journey is slightly different from many and, instead of focusing on scaling up revenue, I decided to scale my profits and time.

I built the foundations of my business for 10 years, and I was well-known in the accounting profession by this point. I had helped over 700 accountants get more clients, and a couple of firms had used my processes to add over 1 million to their revenue in a little over a year. I was nearer 50 than I was 40, and I had bought both a dream house and car.

This is where I made the shift to running a Freedom Practice. I didn't want a huge Monster Business anymore. I wanted to put the fun back in my life. I had chosen to put business first for a long time, so I had to shake up my diary and change the way I worked.

Now my days, weeks, and months are far different from what they used to be.

I still do the CDS Process every quarter to make sure there are not things I can get off my plate. I also have chosen to just offer advisory/consulting services. I no longer have a big team.

I haven't grown my revenue, but instead, I focus on profits and time off.

This is what my team and days look like now. My team is me. I am the coach and chief marketer - people buy people, so it is still my responsibility to show up and be the face of the business.

Then we have Matthew, who is in charge of tech. He runs our all-in-one marketing platform, which is called Uplevel. We sell Uplevel to accountants and bookkeepers.

Twice a week, he runs calls showing people how to use it and helps them. Matthew is a real tech whiz, and he builds our websites and sales funnels. Additionally, he helps our clients.

Then we have Maria. I can't put a label on what Maria is. She might be a bit of an integrator. She heads up operations, organizes the team, and makes sure there is a process for everything. Most importantly, she organizes me! She is an angel.

Last but not least, we have Shola, who looks after the administration, schedules the marketing, and supports clients, too.

The four of us run the business. (Remember, we are profit-focused, not revenue-focused.)

So, with the four key team members, my diary looks like this:

Monday— I hang with Maria. We talk strategy, and we get stuff done. Additionally, I meet with my accountability buddy, Richard. We evaluate how many people have come to our webinars, how many sales calls we have had, and how many sales we have made. Then we discuss anything we are stuck on. This lasts for an hour and is highly valuable. I recommend you all get an accountability buddy.

Tuesday and Thursday— These are client days. This has never changed, but rather than having 1:1 advisory clients, I run group coaching sessions. I only ever have one or two 1:1 clients at any given time.

Wednesday— We call it Webinar Wednesday. I run my own webinar for my audience, or I run a webinar for someone else's audience.

Friday— I try to say that I don't work, but I might book relationship-building meetings in the morning.

However, the afternoons are free, so I can hang with the family.

Saturday/Sunday— These days are mine. No work happens.

Here is the thing. I still create content every day for social media platforms, and the first 2 hours of my day are mapping out my podcast episodes, going live online, and doing outreach to people on social media. I have also opened up my diary for sales calls, and these happen on client days when I am not coaching. It's all mapped out as a time map on my online calendar.

There are two more things I want to add:

First of all, at 1-2 pm every day, I have blocked out my diary for Breathing and Lunch. I am an introvert, and I need to recoup my energy for the afternoon, so I can always bring my A-game for clients. This means I have an hour a day where I will not speak to anyone and have time to think.

Secondly, in the first full week of every month, I do not have any client calls in the diary. This means that for 5 working days, I can work on the business, not in the business.

During this time, I can strategize and plan, meet with the team, or take time off (which I love to do). I can go away or hide in my house, and clients know that I am not as available as I am for the other 3-4 weeks of the month.

This has been the most amazing thing I have ever done in my business. I miss my clients a lot during this week, but it makes serving them even more rewarding on the weeks I show up.

So that's it...I have unpacked a lot here!

If you are thinking of starting an advisory business, and wondering how to schedule your time, and what got me to have the financial and time freedom I have—well, this is it.

In **Dream-Up**, you are excited and are in research mode.

In **Start-Up**, you are in massive action mode. You have to do what others won't, so you can have what others don't. I think a big mistake people make is that when they are in Start-Up or Grow-Up, they want to run their business like a Scale-Up, but this just means they can't get past Start-Up mode and struggle to make money.

Then in **Grow-Up**, you are still focused on marketing and sales, but you are building a team and growing revenue.

Scale-Up, for me, was different. It was about doing less and getting my life back, without affecting my income. Instead of getting ready to sell my business for retirement, I created freedom in my life now.

This is why running an advisory practice is so rewarding and exciting. Unlike a traditional business, life does get easier. You can turn your dream into freedom. I have done it, I have had many clients who have done it, and you can do it too.

CHAPTER 13
FIVE REASONS YOUR PROSPECT WILL CHOOSE YOU

I want to talk about why your clients will buy from you, and how offering an advisory service, and getting people to buy it, is very different than what you did as a compliance-only firm.

When you start to understand that you are not in the business of doing accounting work, but are in the business of helping people achieve their dreams, you can really start to have success with getting better, higher-value clients.

When someone buys compliance services, they are paying you for one thing: to be compliant. It's a transaction that is lacking in emotion. It is there to do one thing: dot the i's, cross the t's, and make sure that their taxes are paid and the government is kept happy.

What is worse still is that most, if not all, business owners do not enjoy this transaction with you whatsoever. They are told by the government that they have to be compliant; if their business is a certain size, they have to be audited. On top of everything, it is the business's responsibility to pay for the privilege. The whole compliance transaction has a lot of negative energy around it.

Sadly, as a compliance accountant, you are stuck between the government and the businesses and are in a lose-lose situation. People don't want to buy from you, so they try to get the best price from you. They say things like, "That seems expensive; Bob can do it cheaper", which leaves you in a sticky situation of always having to compete on price.

What is worse, you might try to over deliver to keep a client. So, not only have you competed on price when you won the clients, but now you have started to let scope creep set in. When a client asks for more services, you end up giving them away for free, for fear of losing them as a client to the accountant down the road.

I saw this happen with my accountant. A few years ago, I asked my accountant (who did compliance work for us) to do some work for our mortgage broker, so that we could get a mortgage. He said "yes", and turned the information around in a matter of hours for us.

When he billed us at the end of the year, he had not included the mortgage work. I asked him why not, and he just said it was okay. Now, don't get me wrong here; my accountant wasn't overcharging us for the compliance work; it was dirt cheap.

He was your typical local traditional accountant who had taken over working in the firm his dad had built. He was charging yearly for services, instead of monthly, and would come and meet us at our house face-to-face to go through the year-end accounts. It was very hands-on, and it broke my heart to see how much work he put into helping us and how little money he made. After working with him for a year, I ended up asking him to invoice me for more money, as I felt like I was robbing him blind because he was undercharging so much.

It would have taken him many hours just to sort out the mortgage for us, let alone the time he spent sitting in my dining room going through the books and getting information from our bookkeeper. I was pleased he agreed to change the invoice, and I felt that the transaction was much fairer when he charged us for the services he actually gave us.

Sadly, this year, our wonderful over-giving accountant gave his notice to us. He let us know he was going to do our books for this tax year, but he was going to get a job. He was winding down the accounting firm that he had inherited from his father.

We have been with this accountant for about 5 years now, and, for those 5 years, I have been trying to help him see where he was going wrong. He was pricing wrong, he was offering the wrong services, and he was running a traditional local family-run compliance-based firm that was just overworking and underpaying him.

When he started his own family and began to have children, the pressure was just too much. Even though I tried to convert him to a new way of thinking, he just wouldn't commit to offering advisory; the end result was him going back and getting a day job.

That is the end of our journey with him. On the positive side, his compliance firm didn't drive him into an early grave; on the negative side, he didn't get to create or grow something amazing of his own. He had inherited a traditional firm, but as a young guy in his 30s, it just wasn't worth continuing.

I see this happen more often than you think with those in their 30s and 40s, who run their own firms but do it traditionally. They start a compliance-based firm, they get some clients, and then they are overworked and underpaid. It has a knock-on effect on their family life; they think about going back and getting a day job.

Now, you might think this isn't you, and you will never return and get a day job. You might be thinking to yourself that compliance work is essential to clients; they won't work with you unless you offer such services.

Let me remind you—the only reason why someone would buy compliance services is that they have to. They have been told by the powers that be that they must pay their taxes and be compliant.

Yet clients are crying out for more support from their accountants. My accountant had so much knowledge. He was so good at helping me when I asked him, but he never gave me any advice without me asking for it first. I drove the relationship forward because I knew both what I wanted and what the questions to ask were. His other clients didn't do this, and he didn't offer advisory as part of his product, so now he is going back to a day job.

People need more from their accountant, and when you offer more, you will get better clients and keep those clients for longer. They will pay you more because you are truly helping them, and they will refer you to others because you have brought them closer to their dream life.

Let's look at 5 reasons someone will possibly buy from you. We will explore how you can describe what you do to attract better clients, without having to focus on being stuck in the weeds doing the undervalued compliance work.

In my 15 years of business experience, I have distilled why people buy into 5 categories:

Buying to alleviate pain—The removal of pain is a key reason why people buy. If a business owner is in immediate and sustained pain, their motivation to alleviate it is increased. Therefore, they are more likely to buy a solution that removes the pain.

An example I could give involves financial complexity and uncertainty. If a business owner is navigating challenging financial circumstances, they will seek out an expert to give them advice and strategic solutions. If they have gotten themselves into a bit of a pickle with their numbers, they will see the value in getting expert advice. As someone who offers business advisory services, do you share how you simplify complex financial processes and give advice around what you see when looking at these processes?

Gaining an emotional uplift— Feeling better is what people desire. People buy products and services to attain that emotional uplift. Buying beauty products, clothes, diet plans, etc., are all uplifting purchases.

Buying advisory and coaching services can also be emotionally uplifting. If the business owner has someone in their corner, they have a feeling of confidence and security that they have never felt before. When you feel good, you are emotionally uplifted.

When you describe your services, do you do it in a way that helps make people feel good about themselves? Or the possibility that your services will make them feel better?

Something we have recently introduced into the Business Advisor Academy is a feedback form that we send out to clients to get their real feedback, not the surface feedback I get twice a week on our Q&A calls, but the really deep life-shifting feedback. The feedback I get through these private forms brings a tear to my eyes many times.

I have been described as a fairy godmother; their lifesaver. I have been told that I have transformed their life and given them their confidence back. This is the thing about advisory and coaching. It is often so much more than the numbers. It is life-changing personally, as well as professionally.

I reckon that if you are currently offering any advisory services right now, no matter how big or small, you are changing people's lives. But in all honesty, do your potential clients know this?

Gaining an emotional uplift is a reason people buy, so share the emotional uplift you give your clients, and you will have more people who want to work with you.

Saving time and money— Your advisory services will save people time (where they try to figure out the numbers for themselves) or money (reducing their tax liability, streamlining cash flow, increasing profits).

We need to be frugal with our time. We need to ensure that our time is valued and that we are trading it for the right reasons. People will buy from you, and hire you to be their advisor, if they believe that doing so will save them time and money.

I challenge you to look at your marketing and your website right now. Do you talk about saving people time and money?

Making money— Almost every business owner needs more money or wants more money. If your advisory offer allows you to make more money for a business, then you will have interested buyers. I see this with my marketing all the time.

If I say, "I will show you how to get more clients and add 500k in advisory services", I get a surge of new prospects reaching out to enquire about working with me.

If I say, "I can help you create an advisory offer", the benefit doesn't seem so great. Even though I know that creating a good offer is the key to financial success, it isn't clear for my buyers.

Money sells. This is why selling compliance is so hard because you cannot position it as a money-making investment. It is just compliance. You need to look at your marketing again and see if you are talking about how you make your clients money. If you are, then you are going to get more interest from prospects.

Guard against loss— We need to protect what we have and what we have built. Saving against catastrophic loss is something we all should do. In an economic downturn, and a contracting market, this is where you need to think about helping your clients guard against loss. I have seen quite a few of my accounting clients have their clients jump ship because businesses are not doing so well in the current economy.

We saw this happen when Covid hit. Companies had to shut their doors overnight. Some accounting firms lost hundreds of clients in a matter of weeks, whereas others grew their firms to have hundreds of clients in a matter of weeks. The ones that grew were the ones that offered a lifeboat to save businesses.

Let me recap the 5 reasons someone might buy from you:

- Alleviate pain.
- Emotional uplift.
- Save time or money.
- Make money.
- Guard against loss.

So now, you need to choose which marketing message to use, which one sits in alignment with what you want to offer, and which one is right for your ideal clients and what they want.

CHAPTER 14
THE ONE WHERE I LOST 1 MILLION POUNDS

Let me share with you a huge mistake I made only a couple of years ago, along with 2 things that you must have to be successful. This chapter is full of true stories and a couple of behind-the-scenes moments that have been key milestones in my business. I hope you see the lessons and that this chapter will save you a lot of stress and worry.

"I don't get it," I said to Matthew (my partner in business and life) over breakfast. "My clients get great results, and I know that people need our offer. So why do I have this nagging belief that this won't work? Why do I worry that people won't want what I do? Why do I worry that there are just not enough people out there who will want my thing?"

Matthew smiled at this point.

So, I carried on. "Why won't I show up and do the videos? Why do I not share my stuff with people? What's going on? Is it that I should just do the content? Why won't I just share my stuff?"

I do this quite a lot with Matthew. He sits down to have a peaceful breakfast with me, and I ask him questions. Tea and toast turns into a mini-coaching session.

He was lucky this day. I didn't need an answer from him at this point. As I was sharing how I felt, I realized what my problem was.

It wasn't that I didn't know what to say in my content. It wasn't that I was trying to sell to a saturated market. It wasn't that I didn't have a good product. It was something completely different.

It wasn't something that anyone could come and save me from. There was nothing external that would enable my business to have the success I wanted. I knew how to do marketing, I knew how to grow a business. What was missing wasn't on the outside.

It was in me. It was two things: belief and faith.

I was living in doubt. I had no faith that it was going to work, and I didn't believe there was a big enough market for what I wanted to help people with.

It was me that was the problem, not my offer or my audience. This lightbulb moment was crucial to how the following years panned out. Moving from a place of doubt to a place of absolute certainty and confidence is a journey. I went on this journey with much success.

However, I had to do a few things on the way.

I am going to share with you how to get more confidence around becoming an advisor or coach, and how to believe that it is all going to be ok and that things will work for you.

People come to me so that they can create an advisory offer, get clear on a target market, and know how to sell and deliver their offer to that market. However, we also have to work on something else: their mindset.

I have spent years honing my mindset to have faith and belief. You need to do this, too.

Here is the thing—before I dive deep into how to work on your belief and faith, I want to share that your mindset is the foundation of your success, but you also need to have a great offer and a hungry audience. If you have both those things, and you are still not having the success you want, then it could well be the mindset piece you need to work on. Just like I had to.

I thought it was my marketing, but it was so much deeper than that; I was blocking my own growth.

Shifting your mindset from doubt to belief in the potential success of your business is crucial for navigating the challenges of entrepreneurship and running a practice.

I spent many years working on having the unshakable belief that all will be ok, that I am on the right path, and that the Universe has my back. (By the way, I still do!)

However, I am not one for relying on the Universe and hoping it will give me what I want. I have to do the work to back up my "wanting".

Keeping this in mind, let's dive into nine points I focus on to give myself the unshakable faith and belief that everything is good; my offer and audience are right.

Point One - Educating myself. The first thing I had to do to check that I had the right offer and the right market was to listen to what they were saying. Not just what the market was saying to me, but what they were saying to other people. I checked Facebook groups, social media, events potential clients went to, forums, and other places.

Developing a really good product offer comes from knowing what people really want and truly desire. I talk to all of my clients and ask them a few things:

- What do they feel they need to make my service offering better?
- What do they feel they love?
- What do they feel is missing?

I co-create with both my clients and my prospects because what I am creating isn't about me, it's about them. I ask a lot of surveys on my media platforms or polls on LinkedIn and Facebook.

I ask my audience questions to get feedback on the thought, "What is it that YOU believe you need to help you achieve your dreams?"

I remember speaking to clients many years ago about how easy it can be to create what I call a *Phantom Avatar*.

A *Phantom Avatar* is a person who you made up; they are not real. You made up their problems, and you made up what they wanted, but they didn't even exist.

I have seen people build whole product suites around *Phantom Avatars* and have never asked their actual audience what their challenges or problems are. This has caused the client to become unglued very quickly.

Here is the thing - watch your community and your audience like a hawk. Observe behavior and reactions to what you are saying. See what people are talking about online, and in face-to-face networking groups.

Spend your time asking questions, and then diagnose what they need. It all starts with you doing the listening—not shouting about what you do.

Something magic happens when you know you have something valuable and that people actually want it.

This is one of the reasons I talk to you about selling your advice and moving from compliance to advisory. I know you want to do it; you know your clients need you to do it; my offer and my audience are a win-win and a great fit.

This knowing is what gives me faith and belief, and this faith and belief are what gives me the confidence to go out and share my offer.

An action point for you is to clearly define who your target audience is, understand what they need and want, and create a product offering that truly helps them; it is better than their alternatives.

Point Two - Leaning on success stories. Before I had success stories of my own, I leaned on ones I encountered in the business industry.

Then I began leaning on my own.

An example of this could be the fact that the thing that gets real results, and immediate results for firms that already have a client base, is the creation of a *Signature System*.

I knew before I started working with accountants that this was going to be pivotal, but I had never helped an accountant set up a *Signature System* before. However, I knew that this was what was needed.

How did I know? Well, one of the most successful accounting firms in the world uses *Signature Systems* in their business. PriceWaterhouseCoopers, PwC as it is referred to, had Signature Systems shared throughout their client offerings.

They had huge success with them. PwC had turned their compliance, audit, and finance functions into methodologies, and they shared those methodologies as packages that their clients bought.

When I wanted to launch this idea into the accounting profession, I had a test case that proved it was a good idea.

I talked about packaging up offers with my marketing clients, and a few ran with the idea; they dramatically changed how they presented their offers.

They got confidence by using a *Signature System* and made way more money.

Slowly but surely, more and more people started to use my methodology to hone their own. Clients went from list pricing compliance to package offering advisory that was sold either yearly (but paid monthly) or on a subscription basis.

Lean in on your successes, or lean in on success you see with your audience and offers already out there, and use that to help you with belief and faith.

Point Three - Focusing on my value proposition. I had to clarify what it was that set me apart from others who served my niche. I had to look at the unique benefits and have the conviction that it was what my clients needed more than anything else.

If you believe you have a superior product to others, then others will believe it too.

This is why faith and belief are so, so, so important; this is why getting your value proposition right is absolutely essential.

My value proposition, at this moment in time, is that we create an advisory offering that sells for 2k a month.

I show you how to create that and sell it to 21 people, so that your advisory offering is making you 500k a year.

Client delivery time for you would be 10 hours a week.

It's a great value proposition, BUT it took me time to hone it. I had to go back to my first point of having lots of conversations around what people wanted, so I could create just that.

Point Four - Adopting a growth mindset. I had to accept that the challenges I was having with my business were always an opportunity to learn.

I think my biggest lesson was when I gave away 1 million pounds worth of coaching for FREE. Sadly, it really damaged my business. It was during Covid, and my *Momentum program* was loved by my clients so much. I asked them what they wanted next, and they shared what they wanted from me.

It was at this time that I started to share the *Signature System* and other strategies that I had not taught in my Momentum program; I decided to create Momentum 2.0.

You know what I did?

Instead of asking my current clients to pay for the program, I gave them the option to upgrade to 12 months for free.

Momentum 2.0 was being sold to new clients for 10k. At that same time, I had over 100 of my current clients upgrade to Momentum 2.0 out of the goodness of my heart. The result was 1 million pounds GONE OVERNIGHT!

I wanted to help, and I thought that giving away my program was the right thing to do. In hindsight, it was the worst business mistake of my life because my current clients didn't pay for the upgrade; they didn't take action.

A lot of people had my information, but they didn't spend the time to make the most of it.

To make matters worse, at the end of the 12 months, I let them know that they would lose access to Momentum 2.0 or they could pay for a subsequent year. A couple of them got angry with me and said it was unfair; they hadn't had a chance to work through the content yet.

In all honesty, it was a really hard time. I wanted to help, but instead, I mucked up my business big time.

So many mistakes and so many lessons. Did I actually lose 1 million pounds? Possibly...

Would they have paid if I offered them an upgrade? - yes, some would have.

Did I learn a lot? - yes, I did.

Could I have been angry and demoralized? - yes, I could have. (Honestly, I was so sad for such a long time.)

Did I make a mistake like this again? - Oh yes! Don't even bother asking me about when I introduced a free high-level mastermind class for my clients. (Do you see a pattern here? I wanted to help so much that I thought I could do it all for free!)

You need to have a growth mindset and learn from your mistakes, and one of the best ways to do that is to look at the lessons from the mistakes, and celebrate the small wins that you might have, to maintain motivation and momentum. (Oh, the irony of that word.)

Anyway, let's get back to how you can have unwavering faith and belief that your business will work.

Point Five - Building a support network around yourself. You need to have a mentor that you can get advice from. All coaches need a coach, and now that you want to focus on adding an advisory offering and truly grow that part of your practice, you must get your own coach. This will help you to know how to run the advisory side of your business.

My advice is to get someone who understands what you want to create and has a value proposition of their own that works for you.

I have competitors (more like peers) that charge pennies for their coaching, and that might seem appealing to some of you–buying on price.

However, if you only invest a small amount of money in coaching, how are you going to know how to command a high ticket amount for that service? You need to model someone who is doing what you want to do and has the mindset you want to have. They need to be further down the journey than you.

If you want to ask for multiple thousands, if not tens of thousands, of dollars for your services, you need to be prepared to pay someone more than $50 a month to learn from them. If your mentor has never charged high ticket sums for their coaching, how will they be able to teach you how to articulate your offer so that people invest good money to work with you?

Remember that step 5 involves building a support network. This is important when working on your belief system. You are the sum of the 5 people you hang around with most, as was famously said.

Point 6 - Implementing feedback loops. Regularly seek feedback on how you are doing with your clients and how your marketing is working.

Data is a really good feedback loop. I get feedback on my marketing message every time I send an email out. I can see if something is resonating by who clicks on my emails, how many sales calls I get booked via email, and how many people unsubscribe.

Social media doesn't always give a clear feedback loop, so please remember that. Before a client bought from me, I would say that none of them had ever commented on my social media posts or liked my content. Most of them came to a webinar I ran, but they were not visible on the social media posts I created.

Make sure you are looking at the right feedback loops. Additionally, when you get feedback, iterate and make your service offering better. Where you start with your advisory package will not be where you are even a few months later.

Point Seven - Embrace mindfulness and having positive thoughts. I suffer from anxiety, and it has gotten worse since I have been peri-menopausal. I find that my daily belief and faith wavers, so being mindful and embracing positive thoughts is a priority!

I visualize success and manage my stress by fostering good thoughts. I look at my goals three times a day and reinforce my business's potential every day; this helps with the anxiety that occurs, despite having worked with thousands of accountants in the past few years.

Point 8 - Set realistic goals and expectations. If you are just starting your business advisory journey, and moving from compliance to selling your advice, I would suggest you DON'T buy into the million-dollar business idea right away.

Yes, you can make a million bucks as a business advisor. I know, I have done it. But that is not where you start. You need to start by making your first sale. Then you need to go on and make the next three.

If you set a goal to have a million-dollar advisory practice, and you are still in the Dream-Up Stage, you are going to be sorely disappointed.

Make sure you set realistic goals and remember, you will overestimate what you can achieve in a month but you will underestimate what you can achieve in a year.

If you start by saying you will just sell 3 advisory packages, and you achieve selling 3 advisory packages, you will feel great - on top of the world.

You will get a dopamine hit, and this will release happy feelings. These happy feelings will enable you to believe and have faith that you can sell more, and then you WILL sell more, which gives you the faith and the belief that you can sell even more.

Before you know it, you have put your prices up and are bringing a new client in every month at 24k for the year. You are making 500k in advisory, and you wondered how you got there.

What you didn't do was set a goal for 1 million and be disappointed that you didn't make it in 3 months. Clear, achievable goals will serve you well when you need to increase your faith and belief.

Point 9 - Stay patient and persistent. This is the final point. Most businesses do not become successful overnight.

It is patience, persistence, and long-term effort that are the key components of most success stories.

It took me 5 years to stop selling my time by the hour; it took me 9 months to go from a few thousand to making 100k. It took me another 5 years to make over a million pounds.

In 2012, I was on housing benefit, but now I live in a house that cost me a million bucks, and I drive my dream car.

I started my business from nothing and now have what so many want.

I got there by educating myself on who was a good market for me and what my market really needed. I looked for success stories and then created my own. I focused on creating a strong value proposition and made my offering different from my competitors. I adopted a growth mindset. I built a support network and invested in coaches and advisors. I set up feedback loops and iterated. I practiced positive visualization and mindfulness. I set realistic goals, and I was patient and persistent.

This is how you have the faith and belief that you will be a success.

CHAPTER 15
THE ONE WHERE YOU BECOME THE ONE PERCENT

In this chapter, we will dive deep into what will get you to be in the top 1% of advisors on the planet. The vast majority of compliance-based firms will never make the shift to robust and transformational advisory offerings.

Here is the thing: You don't have to be the vast majority. You can be the firm that creates an advisory offering, adds 500k in revenue, and sells your services for 2k a month minimum.

I call these people the 1%—They are the 1% of firm owners who take action on what they want.

I know, because I have worked with quite a few of the 1%.

So what is it that they know that you don't?

Honestly, I am not sure if they even know more than you. Having worked with a few hundred firms now, and helping them transition to offering advisory as a robust offering, I can tell you it is not what they knew; it's not what they know; it's something completely different.

Over the years, I've recognized patterns of behavior that separate those who win and those who lose. That's exactly what we're going to be going through in this chapter. So let's dive straight into this and waste no time.

First of all, I want to make this clear. This chapter is not about setting goals and sticking to them. It's not about cutting out bad habits from your life. And it's not about delaying gratification, albeit all of these things are incredibly important to your success.

This chapter IS about doing what others won't, so you can have what others can't.

It is about being the 1% of accountants that become highly successful business advisors, with a great reputation, attracting the best clients possible who pay you without question. It is about generating high revenue, working fewer hours, taking home a greater income, and changing your life.

We need to do what other accountants aren't doing right now to achieve the goal. You need to make sure you are relevant by differentiating yourself from the mass market, and from what everybody else is doing.

You can do that through your service, your unique offer, and the messaging of your brand. Ultimately, you want to challenge what everybody else is doing in this space.

That statement is easier said than done when you first focus on being an advisory-led practice.

I recognize that our very nature, when we are starting something new, is to go out there and find someone we can replicate. We try to find a proven path that we can follow. In many cases, that is the absolute correct thing to do.

In the early stages of launching your advisory offer, find a path that has already been proven. Find a blueprint and stick to that until you get initial results; until you get initial proof of concept.

After that happens, you need to challenge the lessons which you have been taught. You need to challenge the way that you are currently doing things.

When I first started my consultancy, I literally went out to every company in my local area. I was spraying information everywhere! I had a spray gun effect in my local area, where I signed up every single client that I could, regardless of their industry.

I had a kitchen and bathroom showroom, a restaurant (which was my first client), a jeweler, a dentist, and a hairdresser as clients. I worked with local businesses, especially if they were a member of the local Business Network International or Chamber Of Commerce.

The list of clients I worked with was vast, and I may not have given them all great results, but my scattergun strategy allowed me to quickly determine which businesses I enjoyed working with; which businesses I knew how to get great results with; which ones I was able to build better relationships with.

Under these unique circumstances, I found the best path to move forward within my business. It was based on my own personality and my own self-motivation.

What I identified after years of trial and error was that there was a gap in the market for people who wanted to escape their corporate jobs.

I pivoted and started working with people who wanted to take a leap by launching something within 6 months, which would make them enough money to replace their salary.

Over time, I signed more and more of these kinds of clients; I realized the opportunity that I had. Then I positioned myself in the early stages as an industry leader in the corporate escape space. It was great fun...until it wasn't anymore.

I used to run a live event in London every month called the Corporate Escape Club, and we would have up to 200 people a month come to these events. It was my biggest lead generator and a great community. I ran these events for over 2 years and made a huge impact in and around the city of London.

One day my father, who ran his own tax consulting firm, challenged me to come and work with accountants. I thought he had lost his marbles!

I wasn't sure how my ideas and personality would gel with the accountants and bookkeepers, but I was falling out of love with the Corporate Escape Clubs. I took the challenge from my father and started working with accounting clients.

After getting a couple of clients, I saw exactly how much the profession needed my expertise, so I chose to go all in.

I, myself, escaped the corporate world I had entrenched myself in. I jumped over to the accounting profession, and I've been here for 8 years.

I had to think outside the box that you guys have put yourselves in. I was fortunate that I hadn't spent any time in your box, so my ideas were not restricted; I hadn't been trained as an accountant or worked in an accounting firm that had the compliance conveyor belt running.

I came up with the idea to get you guys to create Freedom Practices and do things very differently from how you had been told to run a firm for way too long.

So many accountants, and many of you who are reading this right now, don't break those chains, even when you find initial success.

Yes - Stick to a blueprint that has been proven and follow that religiously; stick to it day in, day out; do the micro-tasks that are gonna get you that macro result.

Just remember: If you want to get ahead of the rest, if you want to get the top 1% of results, if you want to make 500k of advisory services in less than 10 hours a week, you need to do what others aren't doing right now, so you can have what they can't have.

If you are sad offering compliance, working as a generalist firm and offering a generic service, or a compliance-based commoditized service, it is gonna be very hard for you to differentiate yourself and make the top percentile of revenue in your profession.

Now, can you differentiate in a competitive market?

Absolutely!

You can be working with construction firms, for example, and then offer a unique service. Your unique service is the differentiator, and it is a mixture of your education, experience, and essence.

What's next? What do you want to be thinking about? How can you differentiate? How can you go a step further to help your clients? Can you get involved in other areas of their business and see yourself as a growth partner? What can you do to differentiate yourself from everybody else who's working in the same industry as you?

These are the biggest questions that you want to be asking yourself:

- What are you doing right now to stand out from your competition?
- Are you unique, or do you blend in?

Start asking yourself these questions more often. Every single week, you should allocate DAILY critical thinking time; write down 2 to 5 questions based on your current circumstances and the hurdles that you are trying to overcome right now.

You'll be shocked at how quickly you can come up with unique solutions to the issues that you are facing. You will start thinking critically about getting yourself outside of the box which everybody else is constricted to.

Just like I mentioned a moment ago, don't restrict yourself to solely differentiating by niche. You can differentiate through your service. It can be your offer, your messaging, or your culture.

The Freedom Practice business model is extremely versatile, so think outside of the box and start challenging what everyone else is doing.

When you do that, and you come up with unique ideas that you have written down and want to apply, do not go and seek approval from anyone who isn't already in the position that you are seeking to be in.

This is such a fundamental mistake that I have made countless times in my business career. You have an incredible idea, you're pumped up, and your heart and gut are telling you that this is a great idea, so you go and ask your partner or your friend, who's running their own compliance-based firm, "Hey, what do you think of me doing this?"

The minute you ask, they start challenging you because they're intimidated by your ideas. They're not giving you the feedback that you want, and they are just simply not qualified to give you the advice that you need in that critical moment when you need it the most.

It is like going out there and asking a random person for advice on how to climb a mountain. You would go ask a mountaineer for advice on how to climb a mountain, but you wouldn't trust your life in the hands of someone who's never climbed a mountain before. So why would you trust the future of your business and your mindset in the hands of someone who has not achieved that very same thing that you're trying to achieve?

Only ask for validation, or seek approval, from your mentors and people that have already achieved what you're trying to achieve. You need to go to successful advisory practice owners.

This is very important because most people unknowingly will shoot down your idea from their own intimidation and insecurity, with no malicious intent whatsoever.

However, the damage is already done to you– You start doubting what you previously felt was an incredible idea. So make sure you do not seek approval from people who are not qualified and are not in the position that you want to be in.

You have to be prepared to fail a lot when you're pioneering. When you're doing something new for the first time, when you're challenging the norm, you're gonna fail an awful lot.

I've failed countless times over the years in so many different ventures within my consulting firm. This has happened in niche tweaks, in hiring and firing, bad systems, and offer tweaks. (Reread the chapter before this one where I talk about how one offer meant I lost 1 million pounds.)

I have failed time and time again, and I welcome it. Every single failure that comes to me is a blessing in disguise. That is why I maintain a top-tier position in this industry - Failures are not failures to me.

Every single one of them is a lesson, and I am harder and stronger after every single failure that I encounter.

This is the same for every successful person. So few of them had a straight path to success.

You likely know Thomas Edison attempted to invent the light bulb over 1000 times before he found the right formula for creating that bulb.

J.K. Rowling went to 12 different publishing houses over the years with Harry Potter before she finally got accepted, and had someone say to her, "Yes, I'm gonna publish this book."

James Dyson, who invented the Dyson Vacuum, worked on 5000 renditions of the vacuum before he got it right, and people started buying it. Then he became a billionaire.

If any of those people had given up when they encountered those initial hurdles or had taken those failures as dead ends, they would never have become who they are today or built the legacies that they have.

Next time you get rejected on a sales call and think to yourself, "Oh, I'm not cut out for this," or you post a few times on Linkedin and don't get any traction, or you say to yourself, "Oh, Facebook ads don't work," think of those people. Get back on the horse, suck it up, and fail some more. Failure drives the top 1%.

There truly is only one way to know if you are failing or not, and that is by what the data tells you. You have Key Performance Indicators, like how much revenue you are bringing in or what the profit is. This is what most of you will think are the numbers you have to track most, but there is more to running an advisory practice than just the financial numbers.

You have to run everything by the marketing and sales numbers in an advisory practice, too. This is necessary. You cannot run this practice by your gut or through hope. No business can be run by a gut feeling alone, especially when you are testing and challenging the norms within an industry and doing things for the first time.

You have to track absolutely everything! If you're acquiring clients by running webinars, you need to write down every single day how many people you are inviting to your webinar, how many actual signups you had, and how many people then booked a call. That way, you can establish your meeting set rate.

This is something I am very clear on - I know the conversion rates of asking people to sign up, the conversion percentage for them signing up and booking a call, and the percentage of people who book a call going on to become a client. This data is essential for me. I can work backward and fix leaks along the way. Once the leaks are fixed, all I have to do is build my audience.

Here is the thing: Most people ignore the marketing and sales data. They do something once, possibly twice, and then say, "Well - that didn't work." They get fed up and give up.

This is why only 1% of people have success. They 'do, learn, and iterate' over a hundred times before they win. Those who fail have a different way of working: Mostly they 'do, fail, and give up'.

What does the data say about your actions to date? Numbers do not lie. Your gut and your brain do lie to you. Your emotions will lie to you, as well.

That is the reason why you have to track absolutely everything: your cold call data, your email data, your DM data, and your ad results data.

You track it just like you would look at the financial data behind a business (profit and loss, balance sheets, and management accounts).

You have to run your marketing in this way, too. Track every single piece of data that you absolutely can.

If there's a number attached to it, track it, and then get used to analyzing that data weekly or, at the least, monthly.

Cross-analyze between the things that you are doing. Create spreadsheets for the different areas of your practice. We have tons of them inside our program. In the Business Advisor Academy, you have to get used to running your practice by the numbers. It's the only thing that matters.

I expect you may think that I am preaching to the choir here, but the numbers you are used to tracking are different from my numbers.

If you want to have what others don't have you have to do what others won't do...

So I want to leave you with one final question today.
At this very moment, are you doing what 99% of other people are not prepared to do? If the answer is no, get to work.

CHAPTER 16
THE ONE ABOUT HOW NOT TO BE QUESTIONED ON PRICE

This chapter centers around something very close to the heart of many accountants - transitioning away from only compliance work and adding in an advisory/CFO service.

Here is the thing: This can be easier said than done.

All too often, it sounds like a great idea, but you end up reverting back to selling compliance because it is in your comfort zone. You may also struggle to articulate what a business advisor/CFO is for your clients. This results in you not attracting those ideal advisory/CFO clients.

Let me remind you that I founded the Business Advisor Academy. I am calling You out as my ideal client in my marketing, and letting YOU know exactly what we do!
Here at the aptly named Business Advisor Academy, we show you how to create, sell. and deliver business advisory, but there is a big lesson I want to teach you today that you will hopefully understand by the time you are done with this chapter.

This lesson will either make or break the success of getting clients for your advisory or fractional CFO business.

If you get this wrong, you will continue to only attract compliance clients; you will struggle to charge your value because your clients won't see what your value is.

This chapter is all about answering the question that I get asked so many times, and it is: "As an accountant, I want to offer business advisory services and CFO services, but my clients don't understand what they are. How can I describe what I do in a way that ideal clients will understand and want to work with me?"

I smile every time I hear this question, which is VERY often, because I totally know where you are coming from. This is why I created the chapter, "Business Coaches are stealing your clients".

Let's dive in with a quick recap of the question:

As an accountant, I want to offer business advisory services and CFO services, but my clients don't understand what they are; how can I describe what I do so that ideal clients understand and want to work with me?

This is such a great question because it is so true. Most of your potential clients have no idea what a business advisor or an outsourced or fractional CFO is.

If you work with really large businesses, then fractional CFO might be understood. Most small business owners, on the other hand, do not lay awake at night thinking, "Ohh, I know what I need; I need a CFO in my business".

Quite the opposite is true! Most of your potential clients are either living in fear around their business finances—wondering how they are going to pay themselves, their team, and their suppliers; they are frustrated because last year's growth wasn't what they had hoped it would be; they had taken out too much money from the business and now the government wants that money back.

Conversely, they are excited about growing their business and seeing what the future holds.

Most often, the biggest thing that is keeping them up at night is the thought that they have home finances to worry about.

As we all know, the best way to increase personal finances is to feed them with business finances, but if the business owner is struggling to pay the mortgage, the first thought is NOT, "I need a CFO quick, so I'm going to jump on LinkedIn and search for one".

If this is not what they are looking for, what are you going to do? You and I know full well that all the problems they are struggling with are a direct result of needing to have their numbers sorted in the business. What they need to do is invest in a business advisor, or a fractional/outsourced CFO, so they can get the help and guidance that they need.

If they don't even know this, they won't have any idea that you are the solution to their problems. As I have said many times before, they are deciding to invest in a business coach thinking that that person is going to save them.

What is worse, when they are in financial trouble, they start to think about how they can cut costs.

Even if they are not in financial trouble per se, but they are listening to the news and hearing that we are in an economic downturn, all they think about is saving money. They look at their costs and start to see what they are paying money for, and there YOU are, written down on their profit and loss as accounting fees.

If you have priced yourself reasonably, and not too cheap, maybe those accounting fees are a couple thousand dollars or pounds.

They look at this fee and say to themselves, "Right, that's one month's mortgage payment. Maybe, I can find myself a cheaper accountant."

That is when you get the email that says, "Thank you so much for all you have done with us, but we are moving accountants. Please transfer everything to EasyAccts for me".

Then you go through the emotional rollercoaster of having a client say they are leaving you, which takes you through anger, despair, and finally acceptance–knowing full well that your client has made a really bad decision but there is nothing that you can do about it.

You console yourself by saying something like, "They're gonna be back, it'll be okay." (Which they might be one day).

You might also say to yourself, "I didn't want to do compliance anyway" to try to make yourself feel better.

If this is what is happening for your clients and prospects, what do you need to do to help them?

Let's be honest here – the reason you are in business is to make an impact and change lives, so it is your responsibility to get your marketing and advisory offering so good that you can sell it to more people.

If you cannot sell your expertise and your experience, then you are doing the world a disservice. If people do not know how you can help them, and you are not helping the economy and having an impact/making a difference, you will not succeed in business.

It is your duty to get this stuff right and create a way of articulating what you do in your marketing, so you can have more people reach out to buy your advisory offering and hire you to be their fractional CFO.

Here's the thing: Being able to achieve the outcome of people knowing what you do, and resonating with what you do, is all about being relevant.

Relevancy comes from two things:
- Having a deep and documented understanding of your ideal client. (We call this an *Ideal Client Avatar*.) We do this by knowing their hot buttons, which are their fears, frustrations, wants, and aspirations.

- Being able to describe what you do in a way that shows you are the solution to either overcoming or helping achieve these hot buttons.

To do this, you need to be able to communicate with them in a way they understand. Many business owners may know they need help, but they are not familiar with terms like Business Advisor or Fractional CFO Services. They are looking for solutions, not services.

If you are labeling all of your marketing as being an accountant, most business owners have already put you in a box when you use that term. Accountant equals compliance work for most business owners.

So what is the solution? What do you need to do to resonate with your ideal client and be relevant?

For starters, business owners want growth, stability, and clarity in their operations, but they might not know how to articulate these needs, nor do they know where to get help.

You need to meet the business owners where they are at.

Instead of saying things like, "I offer business advisory services", you can use language like, "I help you map out a clear path to grow your revenue and then we make sure you get there".

Instead of providing CFO services, you could say something like, "I work alongside you to make your business financially robust and ready for any challenge".

It's about framing your role in terms of the outcomes and peace of mind you deliver.

While this is a great start, it will not be enough for business owners to truly understand what you do. You need to make this information relatable. The best way to do this is through the use of stories and analogies that resonate with the business owner.

For instance, you could say, "Think of me as your Sherpa in the business world; guiding you up the mountain to the peak of success—whether that's more profit, stability, or growth."

You could also say, "I'm here. I don't want to just offer a service; I want to partner with you through every step and challenge, making sure you reach the top safely and effectively".

When you speak their language and say stuff in a way they understand, you will have leads wanting to reach out and find out more about working with you.

Another thing that you can do with your marketing is to identify the common challenges that your ideal client might have and demonstrate how you can solve them.

One example would be to tell your potential client, "Do you find managing cash flow more like guessing than planning? I can help you turn those guesses into accurate forecasts and strategies."

This approach showcases your ability to preemptively address issues and steer their business toward success.

These ideas are all well and good, and I highly suggest you take note of what I have said about identifying challenges. However, there is ONE thing that you really must get right to be able to get the Advisory/CFO clients—Stop calling yourself an accountant or an advisor.

I just wanna let the penny drop for a moment about what I have said—Stop calling yourself an accountant or advisor.

Imagine this: Right now I am standing on a stage and I have just said these words to you, "Stop calling yourself an accountant or advisor" and then .... Mic drop!

Yep, I've held the mic up high and dropped it! This is a good one, and it will change the trajectory of your success.

Let me explain before your brain explodes: If you call yourself an accountant, your potential clients are going to see you as just that—an accountant. They will expect you to do only what they perceive an accountant does.

If you call yourself an advisor, your client's brain will switch off. This is why: They have no idea what an advisor is; it is not a term they use in business; it is not a term that they have heard very much, if at all...

Instead of using the term accountant or advisor, you need to think about what your client will understand and be drawn to.

This mic drop moment might surprise you, and the reason why you will say to me, "But Amanda, this whole book is about being a business advisor, and you run the Business Advisor Academy. Why are you now telling us not to be a business advisor?"

Here in lies the lesson. You, as the reader, know what a business advisor and a CFO are. If I said to you that I help accountants and bookkeepers set up a consulting business or become a coach, it would not resonate with you.

You would switch off and say, "Naaa! You are alright, Amanda, but that's not for me. What I want to do is be a trusted advisor!"

That's my point exactly—I use the language you understand and know. I don't try and tell you that you need to become something you do not understand; if I did that I wouldn't resonate or be relevant to any of you.

In the first instance, my marketing has to speak your language. For 20 years you have been told you need to become a business advisor by the profession, so I go with what you know.

This is what you need to do with your clients, too. You need to go with what they know, and they are not in our profession, so they do not know or understand the value of an accountant. Neither are they googling How to Find a Business Advisor because they do not know what one is!

That is the bad news, but I also have good news—all the accountants who are not reading this book, or are not my clients, will probably not know this information; they will be trying to get clients using the wrong terminology. When they use the wrong terminology, that doesn't resonate in a relevant manner to people; miscommunication is happening.

This leaves a huge gap for you to swoop in and get the cream of the high-value client crop.

Next, I am going to be sharing with you some ideas of how you could describe your role to potential clients that will help them see the potential value of working with you.

I'm going to give you some titles to start calling yourself, other than a business advisor or an accountant.

How about a *Business Growth Strategist*? This title emphasizes your role in helping businesses identify and leverage growth opportunities.

Another choice would be a *Financial Navigator*: This title highlights your ability to guide businesses through financial complexities. It suggests a role that is both strategic and practical.

How about a *Profitability Coach*? (This one is a favorite!) Focused on the bottom line, this title speaks directly to business owners interested in improving their profitability and operational efficiency.

Here is one a client and I came up with during a coaching call—a *Strategic Finance Partner*. This title conveys a collaborative approach to managing financial strategy and decision-making. You could also call yourself a Financial Strategist.

I'll give you a few more:

- *Business Performance Advisor*: Suggesting a broad approach, this title emphasizes your role in enhancing overall business performance, not just the financials.

- *Financial Health Architect*: This title reflects your role in designing and maintaining the financial well-being of a business.

- *Operational Efficiency Expert*: This one is really good if you are fab at sorting out processes. For those focusing on streamlining operations alongside financial management, this title communicates a comprehensive value proposition.

- *Growth and Profit Engineer*: Combining elements of growth and profitability, this title is for those who use a systematic approach to improving business outcomes.

Play around with these titles.

They are just ideas that I am sharing with you to open up your thinking and explain what you do, without saying you are an accountant or advisor.

Just to make it clear, I am not saying that you cannot call yourself an accountant or advisor ever; being a chartered accountant or CPA is great for credibility; it will help people see that they need you over a generalist business coach who is terrible with numbers and just doesn't get it at all.

Being a qualified accountant or bookkeeper is something that you have worked hard to become, and every year you have to keep up with your CPD and make sure you know the latest rules and regulations.

While this is why you are super qualified to help them, clients just don't get it.

Yes, be an accountant, be proud, and use it to show you are the answer to your clients' problems, but don't lead with it if you want to offer advisory/CFO, as there are preconceived ideas of the service you offer. Instead, choose a title like the ones I have shared today.

Take that new title and use it in your marketing, on your LinkedIn, and social media channels.

Calling yourself an accountant will attract compliance clients because they do not see accounting as anything other than compliance 99% of the time.

Remember, if you think it's about selling yourself as a business advisor, you are missing the point. It's about being relevant, resonating with your audience, and speaking their language.

CHAPTER 17
HOW TO CREATE A LOYAL COMMUNITY THAT WANTS TO BUY FROM YOU

I am excited to share with you the why, how, and where to create a tribe or community and have people recommend you and refer you; even have lots of them buy from you.

Not creating a community around your advisory practice can lead to several significant problems, impacting both the short-term performance and long-term sustainability of your firm.

Let me explain what I mean and what will happen if you don't have one.

Imagine your advisory brand as a party. Without a community, you're throwing a party where guests come once, and have a decent time, but don't feel compelled to return for the next one.

A community, however, turns these guests into friends who look forward to coming back, bringing others with them, and even helping out. This is friendship - or customer loyalty - that a brand misses out on without a community. Loyal clients not only buy more, but they become your brand's cheerleaders, telling others how great your products or services are. Without this, a brand has to work much harder to keep clients coming back.

One of the great things about fostering a community is that it is great for free marketing. Let's continue with the party example, so I can share how this might work.

Those friends that come to your party, well, they go and tell everyone they know how good your parties are. That's what happens when you have a brand community.

Your customers start talking about your brand on social media, to their friends, and in online forums—all for free!

They become your brand cheerleaders. Without a community, your advisory brand loses this powerful, cost-effective marketing force. You miss out on the chance to reach new customers through the most trusted form of advertising: word-of-mouth.

I used the power of communities when I ran the Corporate Escape Club in London. My first event had about 20 people come to it, and, as the months went on, it grew and grew until it reached a staggering 200 people showing up every month to the Corporate Escape Community.

Here is the thing: It grew because people posted about the community on social media and told their other corporate friends. It was an offline, in-person, face-to-face community that I grew.

Let me give you an example of an online community I grew: During lockdown, I created a massive Facebook community of 5,000 accountants, CPAs, and bookkeepers.

When someone thinks of a community, they think of a group of people, often face-to-face or in a town, a village, or a football club. However, you can create a community just with your LinkedIn or Instagram profile if you do it well.

In fact, I have now created a community around my podcast. People are recommending my podcast to others, and reaching out to me on social media daily, because of the content I create.

This leads me to another point.

If you do not have a community, you can lose touch with what your audience really needs. Imagine trying to plan your next party without knowing what your friends enjoyed about the last one.

Without a community giving you feedback, it's like planning in the dark. Communities are great for getting honest, detailed feedback directly from your most engaged clients and audience.

They tell you what they love, what they don't, and what they wish you offered. This information is gold for making your products and services better and staying ahead of the competition. Without it, it is so easy to lose touch with what is wanted and needed in the marketplace. This can badly damage the growth of your advisory offering.

I can share with you today that when I had a community Facebook group in 2019, it was all about getting clients. It did ok, but when Covid hit, my community took off because I listened to the market. I made sure that my Facebook community group gave the direct value to accountants by helping them navigate the Covid business landscape. It grew almost overnight by people recommending and referring to it.

About 18 months ago, the community went quiet. Sadly, as a leader, I stopped showing up so much. I had to pick where I put my energy, as it was limited due to ill health.

I focused on keeping my client community thriving but had to take a step back from the general wider community.

This meant that some people were wondering where they could get that sense of community, as it was no longer in my Facebook group. As a result, they migrated to other communities centered around accounting.

These things happen for a reason, and I am so glad now that it did happen. I needed the space to think about what was the best way forward for me to grow a community moving forward. I had time to think about the podcast that I have now launched. I feel that the podcast I run forms one piece of the puzzle.

This chapter is going to be a deep dive into what I have learned about creating a community and what I suggest you do to create yours. If you want to have a bunch of raving fans who tell others about what you do, then a community is one hundred percent of the answer.

First of all, you need to remember that it can take time to get traction. A community can be as small as 3 people loving you and hanging with you–all the way through to millions of people adoring you. While we probably won't create a community like Taylor Swift, we can create a much-raved about community in the corner of our own little world.

The communities I have run as a business owner have grown and shrunk many times over, and it was all because of how I showed up. A community needs you to be a leader and present. One day, your community might run by itself, but, in all honesty, it needs you to be a lifeblood. Otherwise, it can die very quickly!

When you create a community, you build raving fans. These raving fans help elevate your message, get it to a wider audience, and tell you how you are positively impacting them and their lives. They will be grateful that you are part of their journey. It is such a nice feeling to help people, and I love being a community leader. It is all about doing good things for good people.

The downside of having a community is the responsibility that comes with it.

If you take that responsibility lightly and do not show up for your community, you will upset those people; those who rely on you will be left high and dry and miss you. There is the possibility that, if you fail to keep up your community, you will lose trust with your tribe. This will do your brand damage.

My first piece of advice around creating a community is this: Once you decide to do it, commit to it.

I committed to the Corporate Escape Club community for two years. When we finished the events, it didn't fizzle out. We went out with a bang and it was the right time to go. My Facebook group naturally went quiet when I stopped bringing my energy; sadly, because I had no energy to bring.

A community thrives on energy. Without it, your community will feel like tumbleweed across a desert.

This is my second piece of advice: Bring energy to the group. If you are going to create a community around you and your practice, you need to step up and strongly lead that community. You will need to create and embody the ethos of the group, guide its growth, and foster a space where people can feel valued and heard.

Whether you are thinking of creating an offline community, an online group, or even building a community around a podcast or your

Facebook personal profile, you have to get clear on what you stand for. You need to set a vision.

This vision has to give your followers a shared dream that everyone is working towards. The vision of this community is a Freedom Practice; a practice full of advisory clients who love you and what you do and pay you handsomely for your value. It is adding 500k in advisory services with 10 hours a week in client delivery; halving your working hours and doubling your income. It's highly achievable and what my community is working towards.

My current community for non-clients is the Business Advisory Podcast. We are going to be creating a new online community group soon, but it will not be on Facebook.

I also have a client community. This is something that I recommend you all set up. It is something so special that it sometimes brings me to tears!

Just before Christmas, when we had our last group call in Momentum, I ended up crying right in front of everyone. (Not sobbing of course; that would have been weird and maybe a bit creepy, but tears came to my eyes, as I was so proud of everyone and what they had created last year.) We all had this massive feeling of connection, and we worked so diligently; we all came together at that moment.

Having a client community is a wonderful thing for both you and your clients, and the principles are the same...

When you create a community, you give members a chance to connect directly with your business on a personal level, which helps build meaningful relationships over time. This is because you provide them with a space to share their experiences, which helps them build trust as they gain more confidence in the brand.

In turn, they will feel like they have more of a personal relationship with you and your brand, which helps to create a stronger bond between you and your potential advisory clients.

The reason why most people think of creating a non-client-based community is the possibility of lead generation. It can be an important factor within having a successful sales funnel.

If you are not familiar with the term, a sales funnel is a pre-designed series of steps you get your prospects to go through. It is the start of your client/customer journey.

At the beginning of a sales funnel, your audience starts off as strangers.

During each interaction, or stage, of a sales funnel, they get to know, like, and trust you more. They move through different stages of the funnel until they become a client. Having a sales funnel set up in your advisory firm can be a game-changer, but it doesn't have to be convoluted or complicated.

Now that I have explained what a sales funnel is, let's get back to the community: A sales funnel is part of a community funnel. A community can drive people to be in your world; then they can book a call with you to buy your advisory services.

By the time they have hung out in your community for a while, they are going to know, like, and trust you; they are already fans and want to buy from you, so it gets rid of the uncomfortable sales call. The call becomes a conversation: You find out if you are a good fit for them, and if they are a good fit for you. Then you get clients.

I have gone deep into the 'why' of needing a community. Now you have it. Let's move on to how we create a community around you and your firm. It is a blooming great idea, so let's map out the steps!

As with everything I share in this book, we have to start with your ideal client.

Who do you want to create a community for? Now, this doesn't have to be a specific industry niche, but the members must—and I mean MUST—all have the same vision that you do.

That vision can be anything you want it to be. My community is all about freedom, first and foremost; it's about time and financial freedom.

It is also about breaking free from the traditional way of doing things; it's about the power of being a thought leader who advises clients and transforms their lives, but these are all secondary to the initial vision of freedom.

When you set up your community, ask yourself, "What does it stand for and who does it stand for?" Get these two things straight in your mind. Then you can get to work starting your community.

One of the most common places to start an official online community is through using Facebook Groups, but in all honesty, they are a pain in the butt most of the time for community owners: The members don't see information, information gets lost, and members don't get notified. It can be like tumbleweed most of the time. It's just not owner-friendly.

My favorite online community platform is something called Skool.com. It's owned by a guy called Sam Ovens. As of the writing of this chapter, the infamous content creator Alex Hormozi has now invested in the Skool platform. It is on Skool.com that we run our client communities, and this is where I am thinking of launching my public community, too. If you are looking at building a community for people in their 20s, then Discord is a great place to create a community; you could also start a WhatsApp group which is free; Mighty Networks is another.

My advice is to use Skool.com for client and audience communities; it's the most intuitive platform I have ever used and will replace the likes of Kajabi and Thinkific for courses and memberships, too.

As I mentioned earlier, a community doesn't just start and thrive. It needs a leader, and that will have to be you. You can't outsource running a community; you can't hand it off to a marketing agency and hope they build it on your behalf.

You need to have a strong reason to start the community and then lead it fearlessly to get the group to participate in the vision and mission.

However, you do not need to lead it alone. You can get help and support from community managers and customer support.

Your community will need content, so when you launch it, think about how you are going to attract people to your community. Are you going to be educating people in your community, using it for sharing ideas and starting conversations, or are you using your community to support another part of your business and enhance a connection between your clients?

This clarity on what you are going to put in your community will enable you to be consistent and not confuse people or have the community die before it has even taken off.

Building an online community has become a powerful business model, with McKinsey Consulting identifying 'community flywheels' as the best type of growth business. It follows this flow: People are attracted to the vision/mission of the group; they join and become members; each member gets value from other members; they achieve things they didn't think possible; they become ambassadors and bring in more people. This is word of mouth on steroids!

Here is the thing—Communities can be free, they can be a few dollars a month, or they can be thousands of dollars a month.

It's your business, your rules. The community is your playground. You can decide who is allowed to play in it and what the price for playing your games will be.

According to Mighty Networks, their community owners charge an average of $48 a month and have 1000 members in them; that's 48,000 a month through the community alone.

Having your own community is not something to be overlooked if it fits in with your goals and brings you towards them.

Let me give you a recap of the chapter so far:

1. A community is a good thing to create, as I have already said; it helps you start a movement and can shift thinking and shape ideas.

2. If you are going to start a community, commit to it; it is not something that can be done half-heartedly.

3. Have a vision and mission for the community; there must be something about the community that creates followers.

4. A community can be in a group or a community of people; while Facebook groups are a good community, you can also create a community around a podcast or your social media profile (if done well).

5. Decide what you want to say in your community. Are you educating or starting discussions? Please be clear!

Once you have this in place, you need to launch your community and shout about it from the rooftops! You don't want your community to be the best-kept secret!

When people join your community, welcome them. If it's online, give them a virtual hug. Appreciate your members, and they will return that appreciation with loyalty and advocacy.

If you are fearful and think no one will join your community, this fear is what makes you human.

Some fears are:

- What if I share my community and no one joins?
- What if it's too much work for me?
- What if people are too busy or don't want to try something off Facebook?

It's normal to have some fear around offering a new community. It makes you human.

Here's what I've learned watching hundreds of thousands of successful online communities thrive: The probability that any of these will happen is low.

If anything, with the right strategy and software platform in your corner, you can create a community so valuable you can charge for it, and so well-designed it essentially runs itself.

The key things upfront are to embrace experimentation, stay curious, and reframe your fears into a fun puzzle to solve.

There isn't a single thing you'll be doing in building your online community that someone else hasn't faced before you and overcome.

Your mindset will make all the difference.

Finally, if you want to know what's working, you can ask your members! There's a reason you've built the safety and trust in your community.

CHAPTER 18
CREATE YOUR TEN-YEAR VISION TO GUIDE YOU

I had the absolute pleasure of being the keynote speaker at QuickBooks Get Connected here in the UK, where I met my dear friend from the other side of the pond, J.J. the CPA (fondly known as the Godfather of Accounting). This was the first time we could do this face-to-face, as our previous meetings were via Zoom or social media.

We talked a lot about our visions for what we want to achieve here in the accounting profession, and how we want to help CPAs, Accountants, EAs, and bookkeepers. It was probably one of the most inspiring 2 hours I have spent talking with anyone about the accounting profession. In fact, it WAS the most inspiring 2 hours!

You see, in the US between 2019 and 2021, more than 300,000 accountants quit their jobs; here in the UK, 50% of accountants have changed jobs in the past 2 years. Accounting firm owners across the globe are struggling to find decent talent to fill the shortages they are having.

The American Institute of Certified Public Accountants (AICPA) estimates that about 75% of CPAs would have reached retirement eligibility by 2020. (That was four years ago!)

Coupled with a steady decrease in new students majoring in accounting, it can make you wonder what is going to happen to the accounting profession as a whole. Things are not so grim yet for those of us in the UK. However, it is only a matter of time.

So with this in mind, the way we run our accounting firm has to change. No longer is it a profession that people want to go into when they leave college, nor do they want to spend 5 years studying for their CPA qualification. The rewards are not what they used to be, with firms not being recognized for the value they bring to their clients, and we can still see 50% of small businesses going out of business within 5 years.

Why is that, and who is to blame? Is it the small business owner? Or is it the accountant who is not showing up and helping enough?

It may be because small business owners do not know how good an accountant or CPA can be; maybe it's because you haven't told small business owners how much you can help. You have relied on referrals and word of mouth up until now. You're not helping those who are looking for you; you are just helping those who come your way, instead of having a bigger vision and making a bigger impact.

Now, when I was at the QuickBooks event, I kinda stood on stage and took the problem of 50% of businesses failing to a deeper level.

Here it is—If 50% of businesses are failing in 5 years, can you imagine the stress this has put on the business owners financially? Remember, when someone has this financial stress, it can lead to friction and stress within their family and with their spouse.

Currently, 42% of couples get divorced here in the UK and 40-67% of marriages fail in the US, depending on whether or not it is a first or second marriage.

Come with me on this one—One of the top 5 reasons someone gets divorced is for financial reasons; not only are we seeing 50% of small businesses fail, but, because of this failure, we are seeing a higher rate of divorce in the world. Families are being destroyed.

Who has the keys to the kingdom for these small business owners? You do!

You need to create a vision for your business that inspires you so that you can make a bigger impact and help these business owners and their families in a far more effective way.

You can help eliminate business failure for 50% of small businesses, which will reduce the divorce rate in the process. Therefore, you are making the world a far happier and joyful place!

This is what I want to talk to you about in this chapter: Creating a vision for your business that both inspires you and gives you a North Star to follow—A big idea to get you out of bed every day.

If I can help you think bigger, and have a bigger impact, that is only going to do the world good, isn't it? We all want to have some kind of legacy or something that we can be proud to have made a difference with.

It's funny because I mentioned that you guys have the keys to the kingdom for these small business owners.

I have just realized why that saying is in the front of my mind—One of my lovely clients, Jessica Gonifas, who is a CPA based out of the US, is just launching her new book for law firm owners called, The Keys to the Kingdom: The Simple Strategy for Taking Control of Your Law Firm's Finances to Unlock Wealth and Help You Build Your Dream Life.

That's it explained in a nutshell: She is helping her ideal clients, law firm owners, build their dream lives. She is giving them the keys to the kingdom and making an impact.

When Jessica and I first started working together, the vision for our time together was about her choosing an ideal client and systemizing and elevating her advisory services. We were making sure she was getting paid her worth by articulating what she did through a Signature System.

Here is the thing—The Signature System ended up being a book, webinars, and a step-by-step blueprint for her and the team on how she helped her clients have the keys to their kingdom. Launching a podcast is next for Jessica.

The reason she can do all these things is because the steps and milestones for reaching her big vision (for both her family and her clients) have been put in a methodology. It all started, though, with a vision and clarity of that vision.

I honestly believe that you would not be reading this book if you didn't want more than you have right now; you want to make a bigger impact than you have already.

Here is the thing: Most accountants pride themselves in playing small and not asking for too much from people. The majority don't want big houses, expensive cars, and lavish lifestyles. When I suggest tapping into your vision, you struggle. You tell me you are content, things are ok, and life ticks along. That in itself is ok–until it's not.

It's not ok when you are fed up and exhausted; it's not ok when you work too many hours and don't see your family; it's not ok when you don't step up and help the world as you could.

Creating a vision can at first seem daunting. It means looking beyond the numbers, beyond what has happened in the past, and allowing yourself to dream bigger than maybe you ever had before. It's about looking 5-10 years into the future.

In 2015, I tapped into a vision. That vision was that I wanted to change a million lives. I even own a hashtag on Twitter. (That was a long time ago. Twitter is now called X, and I don't think you can even register hashtags anymore.)

When I was thinking about this, I created a website called Million Lives Legacy. For a while, it was exciting and amazing, and it motivated me. Then I realized it was all about me and I felt under so much pressure. It became about hitting the million number, rather than the change I was making in the world.

I was chasing to get more and more clients every day, every week, and every month; trying to get more and make a bigger impact without looking closer at HOW I was changing the million lives.

Then I came across a particular fable, and it has stuck with me over the years. It has enabled me to hone in on what I really wanted to achieve. Let me share it with you: It's called The Starfish Story.

Maybe you have heard it before, but even if you have, it's worth hearing again...

The Starfish Story, by Loren Eisley, is a beautiful story reminding us that every single person can make a difference, even if that difference impacts just one person.

There are many variations of the original story, one of which goes like this:

One day a man was walking along the beach when he noticed a boy picking up and gently throwing things into the ocean.

Approaching the boy he asked, "Young man, what are you doing?"

"Throwing starfish back into the ocean. The surf is up, and the tide is going out. If I don't throw them back, they'll die," the boy replied.

The man laughed to himself and said, "Do you realize there are miles of miles of beach and hundreds of starfish? You can't make any difference."

After listening politely, the boy bent down to pick up another starfish and threw it into the surf. Then, he smiled at the man and said, "I made a difference to that one."

This is indeed a beautiful story; it is a powerful reminder of the positive impact one human being can have on others.

When I heard this story, I started to slow down and look at how I could help people in a more meaningful way. It was less about hitting the magic number of a million lives and more about something closer to my heart—Truly helping people, not at the surface level, but deeper; making a bigger impact on each individual that I worked with.

Now it's about how I can help just one accountant at a time to offer more value to their clients, but the great thing about working with accountants is that all of you have 20-100 clients or more, so I achieve the Million Lives Legacy through the ripple effect. Every time I help you, you can help 20, 50, or 100 other people.

My 10-year vision is now all about making such an impact in the profession that I change your life so you can run a Freedom Practice and have the confidence and tools to offer advisory, which in turn will help businesses stay in business.

Financial stress will be alleviated for small business owners, which saves people's marriages, helps them avoid health problems, and gives them happy families.

Freedom is what people want, but most of all we just want to be happy.

Visions can be different for everyone. You don't need to take my vision and run with it. There is a vision inside each and every one of you reading this chapter.

Remember, no vision is bigger or greater than another!

One vision you might have is to be the best mommy you could be to your children, which, of course, we all know that great mommies develop great children, and the ripple effect happens again.

Our business vision is based on our future. Your vision has to be driven by you: If you are creating a vision for your business, it is about where you want to be in 5-10 years; it has to be slightly intimidating, but you must 100% believe it will happen.

It has to answer the questions:

- Where does my brand aspire to go?
- What does it aspire to be?
- What impact does it aspire to have?

Steve Jobs famously once said, "If you are working on something exciting that you care about, you don't have to be pushed. The vision pulls you."

I love Harley Davidson's vision: "To fulfill dreams through the experiences of motorcycling".

I run brand workshops. These workshops are part of the Business Advisor Academy program, but I also run VIP 1-day workshops with firms, either at their place of work or over Zoom.

In the workshops, when it comes to getting clear on the vision part of your brand, I ask 4 questions:

- What impact/influence do you want to have on your clients (over 5 - 10 years)?
- What do we want to have achieved within that time (as a business)? What achievements are we going to be looking back on?
- What impact/influence do we want to have on the industry during that time frame?
- What impact/influence do we want to have on our country or the wider world?

They are big questions. They can't be answered in a single sentence as soon as you hear them; you need to get your team together to go through them.

Maybe you don't want to get your team involved; maybe you don't have a team, in which case you can work on this vision yourself.

Align it with what you want and how you want your business to help you achieve that vision. A way you can get clearer on your vision is to write ideas down; and use a journal to write down the answers to the questions.

Ponder for a while (hours, weeks, months, even years). Jot something down, revisit it, and make sure it makes sense and is in alignment, as you go along your journey.

Do you think that Elon Musk came up with the vision he has for Tesla in seconds?

His vision is, "Creating the most compelling car company of the 21st century by driving the world's transition to electric vehicles".

That's a big vision! He probably didn't come up with it in one go.

While it's a big vision, he seems to be achieving it. This brings me back to my vision, and how I am achieving my Million Lives Legacy:

"We aim to transform the accounting profession by empowering accountants to make meaningful impacts on lives and businesses. Our vision is to inspire a ripple effect of freedom and joy."

Not quite as concise as Elon's vision statement, but, for me, I believe it will have just as big an impact on the world as an electric vehicle will have. Honestly, possibly more.

My vision is for businesses to succeed with their accountants' help. Therefore, the business owners are financially well off and have happy and healthy lives with their families. This will have a huge impact on the joy in the world.

I am achieving it one accountant at a time.

Your personal vision is the destination in your GPS (or the zip code in your sat nav); it's where you want to be, not where you are now.

What I have discussed so far is your vision for your business, but what about your vision for your life? Well, this is where creating a vision board can come in handy.

Honestly, I didn't think much of a vision board until a few years ago when I gave in and created one. Something magic happened—My vision board all came true!

I created it in 2018, and on it was a picture of a house on the seafront, a large shiny white 4x4 car, and a picture of Amalfi and Lake Como in Italy, amongst other things. When I created the vision board, I didn't truly believe that any of this was possible: It was more about doing the motion of the vision board creation, as my mentor said at the time. He thought it was a good idea, so I gave it a go.

This vision board wasn't on my computer. I printed out physical photographs. I remember walking to Boots (a pharmaceutical and beauty retailer, not a shoe store) and getting the pictures printed at the photo kiosks. Then I went and bought a large corkboard and pins and stuck these images on the board.

I placed this board next to my computer, leaning against my wall. I stared at it almost hourly at least 5 days a week. Then one day, I was in a position to buy the car on my vision board—a white 4x4 Land Rover Discovery.

Next, I was in a position to buy my dream apartment by the sea. It was right on the seafront with a view like the one I had on my vision board. I followed that up by buying a brand new house, all modern and pristine, like the one I had put on my vision board.

Last year, I took my parents and the children to Lake Como in Italy for two weeks. The location was a stunning villa with views over the lake, just like the one on my vision board.

My personal visions all came true! They were on the board as a dream to achieve; a vision for 5-10 years in the future. I achieved them all in about 7 years.

As I am writing this chapter, it is just dawning on me how blooming cool that whole experience was; from coming up with ideas for my vision board through to making them a reality.

I will be creating my next vision board soon! My board from 2018 has been realized. My initial vision got me here, but now I need to get there. I need to envision what there looks like.

I urge you to create your own personal vision board: Unbeknown to me, it was a truly life-changing thing to create, doesn't take much time, and is so much fun. There is no reason why you shouldn't give it a go!

I have covered quite a lot in this chapter, and I want to conclude by bringing it all together.

There are 3 things you need to succeed with your vision:

1. You need a clear idea of what you want and where you want to go; let's call this your vision. You might have two parts to your vision. Part one is your big vision for your business and the impact you want to make on this world. Part two is more of a vision for your life - like the one I had on my vision board (house, car, vacation, etc).
2. You need the belief that you will achieve this vision; it's about a belief in yourself and that the universe has your back.
3. You need time. You have to spend time tapping into your vision. Look at your goals and your dreams every day, and make sure you are aligned with them in every action you take.

A clear vision, belief in yourself and the universe, and looking at your vision many times in the day is the key to making it happen. I wish you all the luck in the world to achieve what you truly truly want. What your mind can believe you will conceive. If Elon Musk can do it, so can you!

CHAPTER 19
HOW TO RUN AN ADVISORY SESSION USING THE GROW MODEL

In this chapter, I want to talk about your role as a business advisor. If you look up the word "advisor" on Google, it clearly states that the meaning of advisor is "a person who gives advice in a particular field".

Makes sense, especially considering I run the Business Advisory Academy; we are all about being business advisors here.

Well, how would you feel if I said to you that giving advice is not your primary job as a business advisor?

Let's dive into this a bit more, as I unironically give you some advice.

The biggest problem that people in my world have, who are not yet my clients, is fear. They have fear around positioning themselves as a business advisor; fear that they do not know what they want to advise on; fear that they don't know enough to help people; fear that they haven't helped a certain type of business; fear that they haven't run a big multimillion dollar business themselves; fear that they don't know what advice to give.

Then this fear develops into a lack of confidence and they go into a spiral, wondering if they could ever be a business advisor; maybe it is better just to grow a traditional accounting firm offering compliance.

They stay stuck. Stuck attracting price-sensitive clients; stuck doing commoditized work and being questioned on price; stuck not doing what they really want to do; and stuck on the hamster wheel, where the only option is to bring in more and more clients, so they can grow their revenue enough to hire the next team member (for even more clients). It's exhausting just thinking about it.

This fear around offering advisory services morphs into a lack of confidence.

BOOM!

Business advisory becomes a tomorrow thing, not a today thing. All because you didn't know what advice to give.

How would you feel if I said that, as a business advisor, you didn't need to give advice? If you just spent time with a client while not giving advice, you would probably be the best business advisor out there.

Where am I going with this chapter? What am I really trying to say?

Let me give you an example:

Let's imagine you have a best friend, a husband, a wife, or a partner. When you have something on your mind, you decide to share with them how you are feeling. You share how you are stuck with an idea or something that has happened.

You pour your heart out, and at the end, they decide to give you a list of 5 ways to fix this problem. How do you feel when this happens? Do you feel happy and grateful for their advice, or do you want to punch them in the face, because you haven't actually asked them for their advice? You just needed to pour your heart out.

If, like me, you probably love helping others, it can feel great to lend a hand to a friend or co-worker. We can feel proud to help someone get to a solution. We all love giving advice; more often than not, we have the perfect solution to every problem, apart from our own.

Here is the point: When we focus on giving advice, we are often doing it from a place of being ego-driven, instead of an altruistic act.

Let's be honest, most advice is useless. It pleases the advice giver, rather than the receiver; it is often given from the place of what we think, rather than a full understanding of the matter at hand.

People want you to listen, not to talk. Everyone needs help to solve their problems, but that doesn't mean that they want to follow your advice. It's tempting when someone has a problem to chime in and feel the need to rescue them.

I know because I am often tempted.

Unless someone has specifically said to me, "What do I do about ____?", I try hard to bite my tongue and not give bucket loads of advice.

How many times have you heard yourself say to someone, "Have you tried this?" or "You should do ____"?

I have to remind myself continually—Giving advice rarely, if ever, works.

Here is the thing: Many of you have compliance-based clients, where you do work for your clients; you proudly declare that you give away advisory services and help your clients already, but you don't charge for it. Your well-meaning advice never gets actioned, because it is not part of the service you officially offer. You do not ask people to pay for it.

You know the saying, "When people pay, they pay attention".

In most cases, when people say they want to talk something through, they want to do the talking. Your role is to listen, not to take over.

No one cares about your advice, or mine, either. Don't fall into the trap of thinking your advice is wisdom. You can share your experiences or your knowledge, but you can't impart wisdom. It's an internal experience.

I see this a lot in some of the business growth mastermind classes I am in. One, in particular, is led by two gentlemen in their late 40s and early 50s, and they luuurve to give advice, especially to the women in the group; they beat their chests and tell people how to act and what to do.

Even if they have good intentions, it just doesn't work. These guys lose respect; they are seen as the jungle gorillas beating their chest.

So, if being a business advisor isn't all about giving advice, what IS it about?

Well, as I have said in Chapter 5, business coaches are stealing your clients. They are getting paid 1-2k a month, or more, for their services, even though the majority of them have never run a successful business and have never been an accountant.

How do they manage to be a business coach without this experience or the necessary education?

As I have said above, giving advice is rarely appreciated, and powerful business advisors, consultants, and coaches rarely give advice.

Instead, they listen intently and they ask questions.

In this chapter, I want to share with you the world's best-known and most widely used coaching model that will absolutely help you with your advisory offering.

It is called the GROW Coaching Model. It was developed by Sir John Whitmore and is used by thousands and thousands of coaches and advisors across the globe.

The *GROW Model* is a framework that can be used in conversations, meetings, and everyday leadership to optimize potential and possibilities for your clients and for your team (if you want to use it in your business).

It is a great tool for helping people achieve success.

GROW is an acronym and stands for:

GOAL: What do you want
REALITY: Where are you now
OPTIONS: What could you do?
WILL DO: What will you do?

A good way to think about how you are going to use the *GROW Model* in your advisory firm is to think about how you plan a journey. First, you ask your client to decide where they want to go (this is their goal); establish where they are now (their current reality); then you explore the various routes that they could take to get to their goal/destination (these are their options).

In the final step, you establish the way forward, ensuring they are committed to taking the actions they need to take and are prepared for the obstacles that they could meet on the way.

This is a powerful framework that enables you to help your clients reach their goals and make a lasting change towards their success.

As you now know, being an advisor isn't just about giving advice. In fact, you can be a great advisor without ever having to give advice; a powerful coaching conversation with your clients is going to enable them to achieve more in their lives and businesses than you talking through a management report once a quarter.

So, with that in mind, let's talk a bit more about using the GROW Model as a business advisory framework with your clients.

Your job, when you use this framework, is not to give the answers but to have your clients come up with the answers through powerful questioning. This way, your clients will see they already have everything within themselves to be empowered to make those goals and dreams a reality.

Typically, you can use this 1:1 with a person and create a safe space for them to explore their motivation to achieve their goals.

You can use this model to set any type of goal, but in this chapter, we are talking about helping your clients set goals for their business or their life. So why use it in your advisory practice?

First, because the GROW Model works!

It's results-oriented—always ending in the client choosing actions to take.

GROW is also easy to remember and easy to follow, so you can relax knowing you've got the key elements of an advisory session covered.

Once you know this model by heart, you'll find it much easier to stay focused and on track in your advisory sessions.

It's helpful to know that the *GROW Coaching Model* can include a "*T for Topic*" at the beginning—Making it *T-GROW*.

Identifying a Topic (a general area to focus in on) is particularly useful when a client comes to their advisory session scattered and unclear.

Let's go through the GROW Model again:

- **GOAL**: What do you want? (Choose a goal or required outcome for the advisory session.)
- **REALITY**: Where are you now? (Explore where they are around the topic/goal; what's going on for them; and what's getting in the way.)
- **OPTIONS**: What could you do? (Explore ideas and brainstorm what they could do to move forward.)
- **WILL DO**: What will you do? (Identify the actions they will do to move forward.)

When you start the advisory session with a client, you need to pick a *TOPIC*. Otherwise, your clients will be unclear as to what they want and the session will be wishy-washy. A topic focuses the client and makes the session manageable for you as their advisor.

The T (Topic) is not essential. If a client comes to a session knowing (for example) that they want to work on getting more profits out of their business in the next 12 months, then you can move straight into firming up the Goal. You can use the Topic when the client comes to a session unsure of what they need to work on. Or when they're scattered or have several potential session goals to choose from.

The quicker you get your clients to narrow down a Topic for the session, the quicker and easier it is to decide on the session Goal.

Only then can you help your client understand what's getting in the way and help them choose their next move.

Establishing the coaching session Topic often blends with the Reality part of the GROW Model. This is because you may need a discussion based around what's going on in your client's life, to draw out what they want to focus in on.

Let me share with you 4 questions to establish a Topic:

- So, how have you been? (Great open-ended question to drill down from.)
- What could we work on that would help you the most over the next few weeks?
- What ideas did you have in mind for this advisory session?
- What do you need most from me today?

Once you have your Topic, it's time to set that Goal.

Having a Goal is how you ensure your client gets what they want from every advisory session with you. The session goal enables you to deliver value, as well as manage the session timing and stay focused.

One of the things that makes advisory different from just offering compliance work is that it focuses on action and change. It is about looking to the future and not looking at the past of their business. We help the client get clarity on what they want from each session, and therefore ensure they receive value, learn and grow.

When the client drifts away from the Topic (as happens often), the Goal allows us to refocus them. We can say, "We seem to be heading in a different direction here. Your goal for the session was increasing your profits, so what would you prefer to focus on?"

This tactic can be especially helpful if you have a client that likes to tell long stories. It can seem scary to bring a client back on track, but after a while, you will build your confidence and they will trust your guidance.

The Goal part differs from the Topic: You want to get specific! You have a loose topic area, so now it's time to get clear on the specific outcomes your client is looking for.

If you want to uncover a goal, you may need to explore your client's Reality first. Review your client's reality to discover what's bothering them or what would really excite them to work on.

I will share more about the Reality section in a moment, let's focus on Goal for now. Ideally, your client will have one goal/required outcome per session.

If the client wants to address more than one issue, you'll need to make the session goals smaller: you'll need to work harder to stay super-focused and on topic.

With more than one goal, consider managing expectations. You could say something like, "I'm not sure if we'll have time for both of these goals in this session, but I'll do my best. And if there was a priority here, which goal is most important to work on first?"

A goal is what helps us deliver value and keeps the client focused as the advisory session progresses. This ensures they get the support and help they want and need most.

Sometimes establishing the Goal takes a while, and it may feel like it 'eats' into valuable time.
However, a super-clear session goal/agreement makes your time together highly focused. It trains the client to

get specific about what they want, which maximizes client satisfaction.

So establishing the Goal is arguably the most important stage of any advisory session. You co-create an agreement with the client for what you'll work on during your time together.

Here are 4 questions that you could use to help you set a goal in your advisory session:

- What's important to really focus in on today?
- I'm wondering—what you would love to have happen by the end of this session?
- What specifically would you like to get out of the next 30/45/60 minutes?
- What's the outcome you're looking for from our advisory session today?

Let's now move on to the R (Reality). The Reality part of an advisory session is where you help the client understand their situation and how they got there. This is where we question, challenge, reframe, and reflect back to our client what we see.

What have they done so far? What's working for them and what hasn't? It's about really getting into where the client is right now and how this impacts them.

The Reality part of the GROW Model should also include talking about feelings and digging into emotions. You'll also explore beliefs, gut feelings, and intuition. These are often new or uncharted frontiers for our clients.

Exploring a client's Reality is the 'meat' of any advisory session. It is raising our client's self-awareness. We might also look at values, habits, priorities, limiting beliefs, actions taken/not taken, and more. This is where the client gains powerful ideas and insights and learns about themselves.

When an advisory session feels "dry" and functional, or lacks inspiration and insight, it's usually because not enough time was spent exploring the client's Reality.

The Topic and Goal frame-up is what gets explored in this Reality part of the session. In our advisory sessions, we're likely to spend most of our time in the Reality part.

That's because it's your client's understanding of their reality that gives them the motivation to make a change.

It's your client's "reality". How they see their world impacts what they're willing to take action on.

Explore your client's Reality deeply, before moving on to brainstorming Options and committing to what they Will Do.

Here are some questions you could use with your advisory clients to help them get clear on their reality:

1. Describe a day in your life—as it relates to this issue or goal. What are the daily impacts?
2. Where are you now in relation to your goal? What have you already done towards your goal? What have you learned so far?
3. What are you telling yourself that's getting in the way?
4. Who will be the 'winners' and 'losers' if you achieve your goal? How does this affect how you feel about your goal?
5. What has prevented you from doing more/moving towards your goal?

Once we are clear on the Topic, Goal, and Reality, we have to move on to your client's options. If the client could solve their problems alone, they would have done so already, so this is where they really see the benefit of your work together. Often, they need help brainstorming or support to take an action they've been putting off.

This may involve tweaking an existing action: Challenging and inspiring your client to make an action bigger. Or it could also mean shrinking an action to make it more achievable. Either way, a good dig around in the Options section to discover ideas for our clients pays huge dividends.

Brainstorming is a good term to use here. You want to encourage your clients to get ideas out of their heads and come up with as many options as possible.

They do not need to make sense of the options at the beginning of this part of the exercise. They can make sense of the options once they are out of their head and can be looked at in black and white.

Sometimes, the client suddenly sees a way to implement something that initially seemed "crazy" or "impossible". So encourage your client to throw out as many ideas as they can. Additionally, remind your clients that just because they come up with an idea doesn't mean they have to do it.

The best breakthrough actions often come out toward the end of the Options phase. Allow enough time to relax into it, and keep probing them to get more ideas out.

Finally, provide a helpful reframe. For clients who struggle with freely identifying ideas, remind them to focus on what's "Possible" and not what's "Probable".
Here are some questions you could use to help clients get clear on the options they have to reach their goals:

1. What could you STOP doing, do LESS of, do MORE of, CONTINUE doing, and START doing? (Make a list.)
2. Let's imagine it's a year from now and you've accomplished your goal. What steps have you taken to achieve it?
3. Let's imagine you're really excited about this. What would you do?
4. What could you do if you knew you couldn't fail?
5. Imagine you're an expert in this area. What ideas do you have now?
6. What if time/money/failure/what other people thought was not an issue?

The essence of advisory is facilitating change. This usually, but not always, means the client is taking some kind of action.

That's where the W (Will Do) of the GROW Model comes in. Sometimes called the Way Forward, I prefer "Will Do" as it's more specific. I make sure every one of my clients leaves their session committed to at least ONE Will Do.

When I am at the Business Advisor Academy, running our Q&A and coaching sessions, I use the term ACTION and ask my clients to give me one action they are going to implement before our next session.

Remember, if people are clear, it takes away their fear, and this is exactly what we are doing using the GROW Model. We are getting your advisory clients to have crystal clarity, so they can then take action and reach the goals you set with them.

The Will Do part of the GROW Model is the culmination of your advisory session's work. When your clients are deciding their Will Do, this should follow on from the Options part of your advisory session. Your clients review the ideas they've just identified—and choose one or more actions to commit to.

Of course, the actions chosen should focus on achieving your client's stated session Goal.

It's just such a great model and works so very well.

Here are some questions you can finish off your advisory session with to get your clients to commit to an action or two:

1. Can you replay your key options to me?
2. What could you do as the very first step towards meeting your goal?
3. How might you commit to that?
4. On a scale of 1 to 10, how likely are you to complete that action? What stops that being a 10? What could you do to raise the score?
5. What could get in the way of you completing that action?
6. What 3 things could you do to support yourself and make sure this gets done?
7. How would you like to be held accountable for these actions?

There are also a few other things you can ask at the end of an advisory session, to help your clients achieve what they need to achieve.

These can include:

- What do you need from me? (Ask this question to find out what they need from you to support them in moving forward.)
- What was your biggest win of the session today? (By asking this question, we not only reinforce the value of your advisory session but learn what's important to our clients.

When I run my group coaching sessions and webinars, I will say, "What's your biggest takeaway from this session?"

T for Take Away—my version of the Win.

I use the GROW Model in 1:1 coaching situations, as well as group coaching situations. I use it when running my free webinars for my audience and get people interacting with me. The interaction and the asking of questions enable the audience to have transformations in the webinar. Every webinar I hold, I have people say to me how great the webinar was, how useful, and how much clarity they had after coming to it.

For me, the only thing that's not specifically covered in the GROW Model is ongoing accountability.

The GROW (or T-GROW) Model is an "advisory session model" rather than an entire coaching model or process.

In the GROW or T-GROW Model, there isn't anywhere to review actions agreed upon at previous sessions.

We live in a world where it's easy for people to find "more important" things to do than working towards their life and business goals. So, for many people, accountability is a key benefit of advisory. As their advisor, you must be someone who will ask (and check) whether they followed through on their commitments to themselves.

There also isn't anywhere to celebrate actions completed—or to explore and learn why actions were not completed. Unless we explicitly ask, this could easily get missed. I start my advisory sessions with my clients by reviewing the wins and actions from the previous session—before getting into the T-GROW Model.

Above all, remember the GROW or T-GROW Model is not a fixed sequence. It is a framework that you can use and dance around.

Yes, set the topic and explore the goal, but to explore the goal you might find you dance to the Reality section, and then back to the Goal section. Maybe, your client loves to brainstorm ideas and pulls you into the Options part of the framework in the first 5 minutes of the session. They may need this as part of the process for them.

Over time, you will get better and better at holding the GROW advisory sessions; you will become more confident and more relaxed. Remember, these sessions are not there to replace the need to run through the numbers from management accounts or to help them understand their tax options.

These sessions are there to help your clients achieve their wildest dreams and have the freedom and joy they aspire to have.

One final thought: The GROW Model can be used with your team when they are stuck, your children when they need support, and with your friends and family.

As I said at the beginning of this chapter, no one likes to be told what to do. Practice the GROW Model and let people decide what they want to do; your job is to facilitate the transformation they need to have, not to give them instructions on what YOU would do in that situation. People just won't thank you for it.

If you empower them and give them the freedom to achieve great things, their confidence will increase and their life will improve dramatically.

While you will not have given them the exact answer, you will have facilitated, and they will trust you as someone who has their back.

CHAPTER 20
HOW I BEAT MY OWN DOUBTS (HOW YOU CAN, TOO!)

In this chapter, I am going to be sharing how to act and think in a way so that you can have whatever you want and fulfill your wildest hopes and dreams, even if right now that sounds impossible; you spend your life wondering if you could ever do what is needed to grow a successful advisory practice and attract high-value clients.

I will explain who I am and how I have struggled. I am sharing this with you in the hope that you will see that despite how you feel right now, you can do things you do not want to do and you can become someone who can step outside of your comfort zone.

Contrary to what many people believe, I am an introvert. I cannot hang out with groups of people and get no pleasure from noise and comradery: I do not like to leave my house unless it's to go 10 minutes down the road to my office, which is big enough for 4 people, but only has me in it.

I hate sitting in the sun, and I love it when it's cold and rainy. The thought of a laptop lifestyle and sitting on the beach fills me with dread.

Some might say this is a miserable way to be, but in fact, hearing the rain outside and being cozy inside (either on my own, with family, or with a friend) is what fills my soul with joy!

I get my energy from being alone and spending time writing my books, podcasts, or watching movies with my son.

I can converse with only one person at a time. If you put me in a crowd, I will retreat and make an excuse to leave.

If you didn't know me, which some of you may not, you may think I would struggle to do marketing, put myself out into the world, and make an impact. For those of you who do know me, you know I have put myself out on social media, despite these traits. I show up in crowds, even though it is so tough for me, and I effectively grow my business as an introvert.

Even though I have these very introverted traits, I have published over 1000 videos on YouTube; I have run over 500 live webinars; I have spoken on huge stages as a keynote speaker; and I run group training sessions for my clients. Before I did any of these things, I didn't want to do them.

I remember the first time I recorded a video for the homepage of my website: I think it was around 2014, and it was a short 60-second video. My husband Matthew (I don't think he was my husband at this time) spent the day with me trying to shoot this video. Eight hours later, and after a lot of arguments, screaming, and crying, I had a 60-second video that went on my shiny new website. Once it was up, the first person to comment was a friend of mine called Dom. Do you know what he said?

It wasn't, "Wow-I love your video!" or "Haven't you done well, Amanda!"

What he did say was, "I don't like your video; it looks like you are in a prison or something with all those bricks behind you."

That about sums up my first foray into putting myself out there for the world to see. I realized at that moment that if I wanted to have success, I was going to have to manage my mind because otherwise, I would just give up.

Success was not going to come to me if all I worried about was how other people perceived me.

Success was going to come if I could control my thinking through the turbulent journey of running my own business: Some call it being in a state of madness, while others call it being an entrepreneur...

There is one particular part of the brain that enables a business owner to have success. It is part of the brain that Jeff Bezos, Elon Musk, and Richard Branson use to create great things; it is part of the brain that had Henry Ford design the Ford Motor Car; and it's part of the brain that enabled Oprah to take massive action and change her life despite her past.

Most of us, however, don't use this part of our brain enough. This part of the brain is unique to us humans and it is why we run the world. This part of our brain is the VISIONARY mind.

The opposite of the VISIONARY mind is the VICTIM mind. The victim mind is the part of the mind that keeps us playing small and not taking action, or living in fear of what might or might not happen.

If we go back to when my friend Dom said to me that I looked like I was in a prison cell with the brick background in my video; it would have been very easy for me to go down into a spiral and feel sorry for myself;

to believe what he had said to me, and believe that everyone thought like him. I would never get clients.

Then I would never be able to make enough money to buy a house or put my children through college. I could have decided that it wasn't worth the effort and given up. I could have felt bad and maybe even gone into the blame game, blaming others for my supposedly bad video.

What was it that didn't let me become a victim at that moment and enabled me to continue to host that video on the homepage of my website and hold my head high?

Napoleon Hill famously once said,

"Whatever your mind can conceive and believe, it can achieve."

In basic terms, all thoughts turn into things eventually. If you focus on negative doom and gloom, you will remain under that cloud. If you focus on positive thoughts and have goals that you aim to achieve, you will find a way to achieve them with massive action.

I had to tap into my visionary mindset to ensure that I didn't spiral down and believe what Dom had said.

(As a side note, I stopped hanging out with Dom and removed him from my friendship circle not long after this experience: While what I am talking about is managing your mind, it is a HELL of a lot easier to manage your mind when you are around happy, supportive, and kind people.)

This is the way your mind works:

1. Your beliefs influence your thoughts.
2. Your thoughts influence your emotions.
3. Your emotions influence your state of mind.
4. Your state of mind influences how you perceive and act on opportunities in the world.

This means that to act in a way that gives you opportunities, you need to make sure your beliefs are in alignment with being a VISIONARY and not a VICTIM.

We cannot control anyone or anything, except our own actions.

Our mind controls our actions, and our environment controls our mind. Hence. why I had to cut ties with Dom, as hanging out with him would not have had any benefit on my mind.

In 2012, one of my mentors at the time gave me two actions to take to help control my mind. One of those actions was to quit watching the news. This truly resonated with me.

The news is full of doom and gloom most of the time: surrounding yourself with the news on the TV and radio can be pretty damaging.

Now, I am not advocating being ignorant, but I do have the attitude of nurturing my mind with positive thoughts, so I can inspire myself and others, rather than feel life is full of doom and gloom.

I have even taken to not listening to the radio at all anymore, as a lot of the conversation on the news can also be damaging to your mental health.

For example, not too long ago, I was listening to Chris Evans, a famous DJ here in the UK, and he was talking about the price of food.

He was saying how a lot of the food prices hadn't changed, however, the food giants had changed the amount of food you get for that same price.

Here are some examples:

- Walkers have cut two bags of potato chips from its 24-bag multipacks, while the price stays at £3.50.
- Smith's Frazzles and Chipsticks now sell in a pack of six bags, instead of eight, for £1.
- Bags of KP Peanuts are now 225g, instead of 250g, for £2.50.
- Persil now has 75g less washing powder in a box for the same price of about £5, meaning that shoppers now get 37 washes from a pack, down from 40.
- Tesco cut the weight of its 70p mozzarella cheese pack from 270g to 240g, an effective 12.5% price increase.

When one hears this kind of information, you can find yourself moving into a lack mindset and go from visionary to victim pretty quickly.

The VICTIM mindset can show up in your life in several ways. Some examples are:

- All-or-nothing thinking.
- Seeing things in black and white.
- Anything short of perfection is seen as failure.

- Over-generalization.
- Seeing a single negative event as a never-ending pattern of defeat.
- Disqualifying the positive.
- Rejecting positive experiences to sustain negative beliefs.
- Labeling: Attaching labels to yourself and others and describing events in emotionally loaded phrases.
- Should statements: Motivating yourself with "shoulds" and "should nots", resulting in guilt and anger.

Concerning the food examples I gave, these thinking distortions could have gotten a hold of my brain, and my beliefs could have been changed.

- I could have believed that all food manufacturers were giving us less food;
- I could have been devastated and felt cheated;
- I could have been talking to my friends saying how manufacturers should not do these things and how dare they take the food from our mouths.

Oh, it could have been a disaster!

Other ways that you could find yourself moving into having a VICTIM mind is when something happens, or doesn't happen in your business, and these things just make you feel bad: you feel like the whole world is against you.

You might find yourself saying you don't have any clients or that a team member left you. Maybe, you find yourself complaining that nobody has responded to your proposals, or the economy is garbage.

Here is another one I hear a lot in the profession: Nobody is buying advisory services, or the accounting profession is being taken over by AI; there is no way to get good team members.

As I said, it's a downward spiral...

People suffer in a VICTIM mindset for one or more of these reasons:

Knowledge: Most people don't seek the truth in things and have no interest in gaining knowledge and worldly wisdom. Knowledge is POWER, and without it, one will suffer immensely.

Memory: Most people believe their memories about past events are accurate and not subject to interpretation. We believe our memories are fact.

Time: Most people can't associate cause and effect because the two are distanced from each other. Most people seek immediate gratification and give up, or get results but forget why they got them.

If you really want to build a successful advisory practice, you will only stand a chance if you live in a visionary mind: This leads me to the next thing that my mentor said to me. He said to walk around with £500 in my purse at all times.

Here is the thing, it was 2012 when he said this to me. I was currently living on housing benefits and had a lot of help from the local authorities. I was spending every penny I had on paying for a coaching program I couldn't afford at the time. I was living on rice with a Rich Tea biscuit as a treat. I made sure I fed and clothed the children but the rest of my money was spent on personal development. In hindsight, it was quite a fashionable way to live; they call it minimalism now.

My mentor told me to walk around with £500 cash in my purse, and it was for a very specific reason.

It wasn't so that I could spend it on clothes or going out and having fun. It was so that I could get myself out of a fear model. I would know that I had emergency money I could tap into whenever.

The feeling of having money (even though I was on welfare) was going to be enough for my mind to believe that I was successful. I could then tap into a visionary mind and achieve greater things than where I was.

It would have been easy for me to say no to his request, put myself in a victim mindset, and say I couldn't afford it.

I just did as he said, scraped together a couple of hundred pounds, and walked around Salisbury (which is where I lived at the time) feeling like a lady of the manor.

It is for this reason that I always make sure I have cash in my purse, even though most places in the UK don't even accept it anymore, but it does mean I always have cash for a black cab when I am in London Town for the day, and it's raining cats and dogs...

Let's tap into visionary a little more: How do you live in a visionary mindset?

Know Your Potential: Roger Bannister broke the 4-minute mile, and within 2 years, 30 other people followed suit. No one in history had gone before him. He set a new potential for people. Be more of a Roger.

Believe: You have to have absolute certainty in what you are doing and know it will work. Those who have success burn the boats and are all in. Getting yourself into a place of certainty will get you to take action and get results. It's a self-fulfilling prophecy. The poor get poorer, and the rich get richer. I believed I could get myself off housing benefits, and I believed I could make a difference in the world, so I took the next step.

Take Action: Determine what results you want to get and take action every day to get them. I have to say that action is the most important part of realizing your goal. Even when I have been unclear about my audience, my message, my offer, and taking action, gathering data to know what was working and not working, was key.

Then, finally...

Results: We must see the results and success in our heads and the outcome will be inevitable. We must be obsessed about it.

This leads me back to the chapter where I talk about 10x'ing your vision and creating a vision board.

This sounds all well and good, but how do you switch from having the victim mindset to being a visionary?

Here are some examples of how we can move from the negative to the positive:

- Change "I was born this way, nothing I can do about it" to "I can improve because skills come from hard work".
- Stop saying, "This is challenging; I will avoid it: I won't be able to do it anyway". Instead, say, "This will allow me to grow. I will be more persistent".
- Switch "It's not worth putting the effort in" to "This effort is essential; I will be on the path to mastery!"
- Avoid thinking, "I don't want feedback; I feel persecuted". Instead, think, "This feedback is useful; I can learn from it and see where to improve".
- Refuse to think, "It's not my fault" and go with "Next time I will smash it".

Here is the kicker, whether you think you can or you can't, you are right. You have to change your mindset or keep it where it is, but it all starts with you.

As I move on to the final section of this chapter, let's talk about leveling up your mindset with three actions I take every single day:

BE AWARE OF YOUR SELF-TALK AND CHANGE IF NECESSARY. The conversations you have with yourself are a direct reflection of your mindset. If you are telling yourself, "I am not good enough to achieve my dreams", your thoughts will create your reality. Your mindset will hold you back from having the life you want.

In order to upgrade your mindset, change your negative self-talk to an empowerment speech. Sounds cliché, but telling yourself "I can do this" or "I got this", really works.

DETERMINE THE MINDSET. YOU NEED TO ACT "AS IF". Pick a goal you want to achieve and ask yourself, "Which mindset do I need to achieve this goal?" and "Which mindset do people have that were successful at this goal?".

For example, healthy & fit people might share the mindset, "I love taking care of my body, nourishing it with whole foods, and exercising every day".

If it's your goal to be healthy & fit, act as if you already HAVE the mindset of a healthy & fit person. This way, you are tricking your brain into adopting a new mindset and reinforcing it with action.

JUMP OUT OF YOUR COMFORT ZONE. If you put yourself in situations that challenge you, you have no other choice than to rise to the occasion and upgrade your mindset.

It becomes a necessity to survive.

Ask yourself, "What situations can I put myself in that will require me to operate on a higher mindset?".

The idea is to engineer your environment to train your brain!

I came across this poem the other day. I will share it with you now to wind up this chapter, and this volume of the Business Advisor Playbook.

Thinking
Written by Walter D. Wintle

If you think you are beaten, you are;
If you think you dare not, you don't.
If you like to win, but you think you can't.
It is almost certain you won't.

If you think you'll lose, you're lost.
For out of the world we find
Success begins with a fellow's will-
It's all in the state of mind.

If you think you are outclassed, you are;
You've got to think high to rise;
You've got to be sure of yourself before
You can ever win a prize.

Life's battles don't always go
To the stronger or faster man;
But soon or later the man who wins,
Is the man WHO THINKS HE CAN!

NEXT STEPS

SUBSCRIBE TO THE BUSINESS ADVISOR PODCAST
https://BusinessAdvisorPodcast.com

SUBSCRIBE TO OUR YOUTUBE CHANNEL
https://youtube.com/@AmandaCWatts

JOIN "THE FREEDOM TRIBE" - an online group where you can mingle and learn alongside your peers on how to market and sell a high-value advisory offering
https://BusinessAdvisorAcademy.com/TheFreedomTribe

LIVE EVENTS/WORKSHOPS - A few times a year you will find us LIVE in the UK, USA or Australia. Keep an out for all the details on our website
https://BusinessAdvisorAcademy.com

THE BUSINESS ADVISOR ACADEMY - when you are ready to embrace the game of being a business advisor book a call to speak with one of our team and see if we are a good fit.
https://info.businessadvisoracademy.com/talk-to-coach

The Business Advisor Academy is ideal for partners and practice owners who want to launch or scale a Business Advisory/CFO offer.

I hope I get to meet some of you soon – either at a workshop or in the Business Advisor Academy. In the meantime, please do spread the word about this book and our podcast.

Thank you so much for being part of my world and I wish you and your firm every success.

If there's ever anything I can do, just let me know!

If you think it's about creating a business advisory practice you're missing the point; it's about creating a life of freedom.

ABOUT AMANDA C. WATTS

Amanda is a passionate strategist for business advisors and the driving force behind the Business Advisor Academy and Oompf Global.

As the co-founder of Uplevel By Oompf and an engaging keynote speaker, she thrives on inspiring and connecting with her audience. Amanda's mission is to help CPAs, accountants, bookkeepers, financial coaches, and business coaches across the globe become not only wildly wealthy but also impactful advisors.

With over a decade of experience since 2009, Amanda has empowered more than 3000 practices in 23 countries, guiding some of the fastest-growing, award-winning accounting firms. She is also a prolific author with three books (and a fourth on the way) focused on branding, marketing, and sales.

She firmly believes that business advisory is crucial in today's world, especially for small businesses seeking to thrive with the right financial guidance.

Amanda is committed to transforming practices into beacons of success and influence, making a significant difference in the business world.

ABOUT THE BUSINESS ADVISOR ACADEMY

Founded by Amanda C Watts, the Business Advisor Academy is designed specifically for accountants and finance professionals looking to expand their services into business advisory and CFO roles. The Academy offers practical training, essential tools, and ready-to-use templates to help students effectively create, sell, and deliver these services.

At the Business Advisor Academy, our students gain access to a suite of resources that support the implementation of the Business Advisor Methodology. Beyond resources, our community provides a network of peers who share the same professional path. Members benefit from regular support sessions, including Q&A opportunities, mastermind groups, and accountability check-ins.

www.ingramcontent.com/pod-product-compliance
Lightning Source LLC
Chambersburg PA
CBHW052141220526
45471CB00004B/1473